REGICIDE

JOHN WORTHEN

Regicide

The Trials of Henry Marten

Published in 2022 by
Haus Publishing Ltd
4 Cinnamon Row
London SW11 3TW

Copyright © John Worthen, 2022

A CIP catalogue for this book is available from the British Library

The moral right of the author has been asserted

ISBN 978-1-913368-35-7
eISBN 978-1-913368-36-4

Typeset in Sabon by MacGuru Ltd

Printed in the UK by Clays Ltd, Elcograf S.p.A.

www.hauspublishing.com
@HausPublishing

For Moyra Tourlamain

Contents

Note on Language, Sources, Dates, and Abbreviations

In period quotations, to assist the modern reader, 'ʃ' for 's' and 'J' for 'I' have been silently adjusted, the punctuation occasionally very slightly modified and bold face awarded to speakers' names in the trial transcripts; italics present in original texts have been retained in quotations; modern spelling has in general only been adopted where the reader might momentarily be nonplussed (for example, by non-standard forms such as 'haz' and 'fewel'). New Year's Day was celebrated on 25 March in the seventeenth century, but dates have been adjusted to fit a year starting on 1 January (the execution of Charles I, for example, occurred on 30 January 1648 in seventeenth-century dating but on 30 January 1649 in modern dating). Lockdowns and library restrictions are responsible for more references to non-MS sources than I would have wished. Printed books frequently cited in the text are supplied with page references. Place of publication, here and elsewhere, is London unless otherwise stated.

Coxe   William Coxe, *An Historical Tour in Monmouthshire; Illustrated with Views by Sir R. C. Hoare, Bart.*, 2 Vols. (1801)

EIA   *An Exact and most Impartial Accompt of the Indictment, Arraignment, Trial, and Judgment (According to Law) of Twenty Nine Regicides* (1660)

L   *Coll. Henry Marten's Familiar Letters to His Lady of Delight* (Oxford, 1662)

Illustrations

Acknowledgements

I came across Henry Marten in 1969 and have been wondering for fifty years why so few people were interested in this fascinating, articulate man. Sarah Barber and John Rees are the only scholars since C. M. Williams to have published much serious work on Marten, but I have done what I can to make sense of the chaotic state of Marten's surviving letters to Mary Ward: I have used them to illuminate his life in the Tower of London during his trials. I want also to acknowledge the help given me by the Chepstow Society, Harry Hall, Alice Horne, and Jo Stimfield; by Grant Lewis (to whom I owe the location of Illustration 9) and Anne Rainsbury (of great help with Illustrations 5 and 15, and in locating a surviving fragment of Marten's tombstone); and by Linda Bree, David Ellis, Caroline Murray, Cornelia Rumpf-Worthen, and Simon Smith.

'We are the men of the present age'

'Regicide: the killing or murder of a king.' Charles I, King of England, had been executed on 30 January 1649, following the first ever trial of an English king, staged in Westminster Hall in the old Palace of Westminster. Whether it had been a killing or a murder was disputed at the time and has been ever since.[1] The trial had, for sure, not been conducted in the usual way of English trials with a judge and jury, but with a president (the lawyer and MP John Bradshaw, wearing a metal-lined hat in case anyone took a gun, sword, or pike to him) and over sixty so-called commissioners. The majority were MPs, many of them until recently in the army, but with a hard core of army officers also attending regularly, 'giving some justification to the charge that proceedings were by court martial'.[2] The most famous representation of this High Court of Justice, banked up high around their president, was, however, first published thirty-five years later, its layout designed to fit the page of the book in which it first appeared. It effectively halved the actual width of Westminster Hall, turning a landscape picture into a portrait appropriate for a book. Quite another version of how Westminster Hall looked during the trial is presented in a drawing which not only takes account of (although slightly exaggerates) the astonishing width of the hall (sixty-seven feet) and the sheer tumultuous presence of so many people but allows for the commissioners to be seated in three rows along the flight of three steps that leads up to the

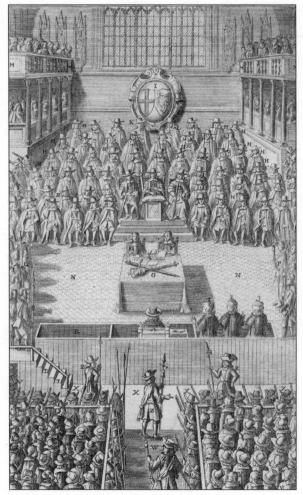

Illustration 1: Trial of Charles I: engraving, *c*. 1684

great window at the end of the hall. Although the artist had problems with perspective and galleries, the result offers an image far more vivid and probably more accurate.

The artist confirms the military setting of the whole: two hundred guards were on duty, and the picture shows soldiers everywhere, including those with flags at the front.

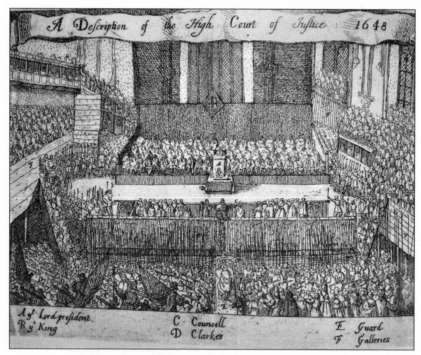

Illustration 2: Trial of Charles I: ink drawing, 1649

For (to quote one of the great early historians of the period), 'It was not the revolutionary tribunal over which Bradshaw presided that condemned King Charles to death. What it did was to put into legal language the verdict the Army had pronounced.'[3] After its victories in the Civil War, the Parliamentarian Army had, to all intents and purposes, come to power in 1648, and Major General Henry Ireton, an extraordinarily able young politician and general (he had fought at Edgehill, Marston Moor, Newbury, and Naseby), had driven forward the trial and the eventual condemnation of the king. He had led a 'resolute minority' of army grandees who, in turn, had 'canalised the passions of 30,000 men of action',[4] and – to start with – men like Ireton passionately believed that the monarchy would soon be replaced by a more representative and more regularly elected parliament. This enterprise would run in parallel to the army's needs and wishes, because the army's commanders were also politicians: men like the indefatigable Ireton and also Oliver Cromwell. They were able to channel the excitement which characterised those in the army and outside it who had come to believe that

> whatever our Fore-Fathers were; or whatever they did or suffered, or were enforced to yeeld unto; we are the men of the present age, and ought to be absolutely free from all kindes of exorbitancies, molestations or *Arbitrary Power* ...[5]

Henry Marten, who is going to be centre stage throughout this book, was without question one of 'the men of the present age'. Illustrations 1 and 2 show him at the height of his political responsibility as one of the commissioners at the king's trial, sitting directly under the shield at the back;[6] the man beside him, according to the 1684 engraver (who added the letters 'K' and 'L'), is Cromwell. Marten, as an MP in 1643, had not only been censured by the House of Commons (led by the pivotal Puritan John Pym) for anti-monarchist sentiments but had been committed by them to the Tower of London and expelled from the Commons for three years. In January 1649 he was nevertheless able to come up with the crucial form of words for which the group of men organising the king's prosecution had been asking:

> ... *by what Authority and Commission do we try him? To which none answered presently. Then after a little space* Henry Marten ... *rose up, and said, in the name of the Commons and Parliament assembled, and all the good People of England, which none contradicted* ... (EIA 248)

That is the most famous thing that Marten is reported ever to have said (see also pages 92–3). But he was a man renowned in parliament for his sense and quick-wittedness.

Marten (army colonel from 1643) was not only one of the group that had steered through the king's trial and execution he was then on the Council of State which took control of the country. In January 1649, too, he had chaired the Commons committee that had produced the new credo of republicanism:

> Resolved, &c. That the Commons of England, in Parliament assembled, do Declare, That the People are, under God, the Original of all just Power: And do also Declare, that the Commons of England, in Parliament assembled, being chosen by, and representing the People, have the Supreme Power in this Nation ...[7]

'For we' – Marten could have added – 'are the men of the present age.' The declaration continued:

> And do also Declare, That whatsoever is enacted, or declared for Law, by the Commons, in Parliament assembled, hath the Force of Law; and all the People of this Nation are concluded thereby, although the Consent and Concurrence of King, or House of Peers, be not had thereunto.

And, to end this brief catalogue, Marten was the man who came up with the wording on the first ever Great Seal of England (used to add authenticating wax seals to state documents) neither to display the monarch's image nor to employ Latin: he was responsible for the first inscription in English that the seal had borne in six hundred years (see pages 133–6). As so often, it was Marten who did the words: in this case radical, transforming words.

※

It must have been around 1649–50, at the height of Marten's political responsibility, that – along with other important people on the ruling council – his portrait was painted by ex-court artist Sir Peter Lely. His nose appears very large, his chin marked, his air gently supercilious. The antiquary John Aubrey – who writes as if he had met Marten – would note, 'his habit moderate: his face not good', while Charles I is supposed to have called him 'that ugly Rascall'. The black cap he wears, though, is stylish, as is a glinting brooch-like jewel at his neck.[8] His hair is long, his moustache turned up, his eyebrows apparently permanently raised, his eyes penetrating and large: his whole face on the verge of a smile but not indulging it.

Especially striking is a comparison with the portrait of Cromwell that Lely painted at around the same time: the picture of a tough politician and soldier, clean-shaven, face ruddy and outdoors, the wart (just the one) very clear, but the whole conception dominated by the reflection of his armoured shoulder-piece and breast-plate. That is what shines and glints in his portrait, not a jewel; Cromwell (with Lely's help) presents himself entirely as a down-to-earth soldier. Marten, however, repudiates his roles as colonel and politician to be an almost monkish, elegant, indoors eminence – still ironical about everything. Even the contemporary inscription 'now' in gold that hovers by his face (enhancing the portrait, not defacing it[9]) is a fine and ironical reminder of the precariousness of status and power. Again it is Marten who does the words: this is how he now is, but goodness knows how, later on, he might be. As he would later tell his mistress Mary Ward, he was 'Thy H. M. now' (*L* 17). What more could anyone offer?

And indeed, the republican enterprise, along with Marten's public career, ran into the sand over the next few years; by the

Illustration 3: Henry Marten: oil painting by Peter Lely, *c.* 1650

end of 1653 Cromwell had accepted the role of Lord Protector, working with a written constitution and in theory supported by 'the people assembled in Parliament' but, in fact, kept in position by a standing army. He ended up as king in all but name, using his own 'high hand of Arbitrary power' to control parliament, army, and country. When he died rather suddenly in 1658 there followed an eighteen-month crisis which led to the Restoration.[10] Cromwell's son Richard – after setting in train quarrels between parliament and army in which he was helpless to exert power – quickly abandoned the enterprise he had been gifted, and sections of the army, supported by members of the House of Commons, resolved upon a restoration of the monarchy by acquiring the appropriate royal personage. This was Charles I's son, who was in Holland watching events intently. One army general, George Monck, took more responsibility on himself than any other, and those who supported him found themselves happily in the ascendant when Monck brought Charles back. Those who still believed in the Commonwealth were desperate over the failure of the revolutionary republican enterprise, which they called the 'Good Old Cause' or 'the Common Cause'[11] or simply 'the Cause'. But they were left to cope as best they could.

※

Before leaving Holland Charles had issued a declaration indemnifying those who had governed without him and had fought against his father. There was initially a single set of exceptions to those pardoned: the men who had been directly responsible for his father's execution. These men – the term 'regicides'[12] was quickly applied to them, and it has stuck – were criminalised for committing high treason. The group included all those who had sat in the High Court of Justice and had signed the warrant for Charles's execution as well as those who had taken him on to the scaffold and various others deemed directly responsible for his death.

Events moved quickly in May 1660. On the 1st Charles's Declaration of Breda was read in the remnants of the old parliament, known as the Rump, members having already 'voted our late King's death to be murder'.[13] A week later parliament declared

Illustration 4: Oliver Cromwell: oil painting by Peter Lely, 1650

Charles to have been king since 30 January 1649, and two weeks after that it ordered the arrest of the regicides, who were obliged to hand themselves in to the Serjeant at Arms of the House of Commons by 20 June. An enterprising printer rushed out a pamphlet (*A Hue and Cry After the High Court of Injustice*) on 22 May, before the king even returned to England, stressing what in royalist quarters was now being demanded, that 'those Blood-thirsty and unparallel'd Traitors' responsible in 1649 for the 'High Court of Injustice' should be hunted down and 'made publick Examples of Justice', the pamphlet's title page carrying biblical justification for their deserved 'Ruine and Destruction': 'ye shall take no satisfaction for the life of a Murderer which is guilty of Death, but he shall surely be put to death' (Numbers xxxv. 31) – one of the passages previously used to justify the execution of Charles I.

Charles, arguably returning because both army and parliament wanted him to (one MP hopefully commented that it was the 'Representative Body of *England*' that was actually responsible for bringing him back), finally arrived in England on 29 May 1660. Amid the disruption to all the forms of government and organisation then under way, many of the regicides had already taken action. Some had gone into exile on the Continent; some indeed, foreseeing what was coming, had left weeks earlier. The *Hue and Cry* pamphlet had proclaimed, under the 'O yes!' of the public Cryer, that

> If any man or Woman, in City, Town, or Countrey, can Discover, or bring Tydings of any of these aforesaid Traytors who are fled away: Let them convey them safe to the Tower of *London,* and they shall be well rewarded for their Pains ...[14]

... the Tower being the prison for those facing the charge of treason. The majority of those who left went to Holland, Germany, and Switzerland, but three ended up in New England; at least one went into exile but came back; one was murdered abroad by royalist sympathisers. Some consulted with friends and colleagues about what would be best to do, others handed themselves in following the demand of the House of Commons that they do so (Henry Marten – again a loyal member of

the House – was one of those). Still others were ignomini-
ously arrested; one (the preacher Hugh Peters) managed to
conceal himself until 2 September before being found. The
career soldier Francis Hacker was tricked into believing himself
safe and lived securely at his own house until, being summoned
to London, he was seized; the wealthy merchant Gregory Cle-
ments, hidden in a house in Purple Lane near Gray's Inn, might
have escaped but for his rather remarkable voice being recog-
nised by a blind man.

A country undergoing a complete change in the way in which
it was run took a little time before it was ready to deal with
men who had been turned almost overnight from its leaders
and authorities into its criminals. As late as the end of June, for
example, nothing could be done about the regicides 'because
the Courts of justice are not filled, nor are either of the Chief
justices as yet appointed'.[15] However, an immensely confused
and complex sequence of negotiations in parliament – now
restored to being one of the real powers in the land – occurred
between May and August: one MP wrote graphically in June
how 'The trial of the regicides takes up most of the time of
both Houses',[16] as both Commons and Lords saw themselves
as, in effect, operating as courts of justice. Battles were fought
out within each House over the names of those who should be
added to or deleted from the crucial list. Scores were settled,
friendships celebrated, deals done: another MP wrote in
June how

> The weather is not so hot, but the debates in the House equal
> it in warmth; several persons guilty enough to bring them
> within the exceptions [i.e. those excepted from the 'Bill of Free
> and General Pardon, Indemnity, and Oblivion', to give its full
> title] finding friends enough to excuse them ...[17]

For the crucial decisions depended not only on who exactly might be defined as a regicide but on who had friends (or enemies) in the Houses of Parliament. Four commissioners, for example – including one, Thomas Wogan, who had actually signed the death warrant and had also presented himself a week late to the Serjeant at Arms – were imprisoned but were not sent to be tried for high treason.

The negotiations between Commons and Lords took even longer, were more complex and at times more contentious and bad-tempered; 'they have not always parted like brethren', wrote one MP, sadly. 'The account between the Houses of Parliament comes off with discord.' At some points indeed, it appeared that the House of Lords was still in favour of 'taking away the lives of all the King's Judges',[18] thus ignoring the problem of the regicides who had surrendered themselves to the House of Commons back in June. Confronted by the Lords' determination to condemn individuals whom the Commons wanted to save, solicitor general Finch urged the Commons not 'to venture the shipwreck of the whole vessel [rather] than throw a few overboard',[19] and by 24 August a compromise conclusion had been reached in a conference between the two Houses. A new Act of Parliament would have to be passed to deal with those who had surrendered. Nevertheless,

> The Conference being about to break off, *the Lord Northampton said, That these* Regicides came in upon the Proclamation, because Nobody durst harbour them, and no way else.

Conscious of the Act of Parliament he wanted, which would condemn them all, James Compton, 3rd Earl of Northampton – the regicide and republican Edmund Ludlow believed him 'a great favourite of Monke's'[20] – angrily insisted 'That the stopping [hindering of] this Act was sparing the King's Murderers'. He wanted revenge and felt in danger of not getting it; he had previously got one regicide off the hook (Richard Ingoldsby: see pages 80–1) but was here distinguishing between those he thought repentant and those he believed simply trying to evade punishment.

And although the Houses of Parliament were, in theory, doing no more than ensuring that – in the words of the diarist, royalist, intellectual, and scholar John Evelyn – 'those barbarous *Regicides*, who sat on the life of our late King'[21] were sent for trial at the Old Bailey courthouse, in central London, many MPs already saw such a trial as being no more than a formality: they believed that they were taking the crucial decisions. Colonel Daniel Axtell, for example, who had commanded some of the guards in Westminster Hall during the king's trial, was excepted from pardon, a member of the Commons remarking confidently in August, weeks before the Old Bailey trial took place, that 'Axtell, who was lately brought out of Ireland, shall be hanged and quartered'.[22] Another individual, Colonel Adrian Scrope, was – according to the desire and say-so of one significant enemy – singled out by parliament for execution.

On the other hand, although it has been stated as 'remarkable' that a man such as Henry Marten 'had not been included in the primary death list' and that 'His omission seems to have been due only to sheer weight of numbers',[23] that was not the case. There never had been a 'primary death list' and numbers had never been a problem. The House of Commons had simply resolved on 17 May 1660

that all the Persons who sat in Judgment upon the late King's Majesty, when Sentence of Death was pronounced against him, and the Estates both real and personal, of all and every the said Persons, whether in their own Hands, or in the Hands of any other, in Trust for their or any of their Uses, who are fled, be forthwith seized and secured ...

Over the weeks it had added various other people to the list of those to be seized, such as the clerks who had worked at the king's trial. It simply assumed from the start that all those secured would be put on trial for treason. The names on the list were what mattered: that was what had to be negotiated.

※

The Old Bailey Trial was staged in October 1660 to outdo the events of January 1649 in authority and in significance. It was designed to take a terrible, public, and deliberate revenge upon those 'immediately guilty of that Murder of My Father', as Charles II phrased it,[24] and to show how the history of the previous eleven years had now been rewritten to suit the new rulers' narrative – at times literally so, as in the declaration that Charles II had been king since 30 January 1649.[25] And the trial was also to demonstrate bloodily – and terrifyingly – how matters were now to be resolved. The regicides would not, however, be tried in the grand spaces of Westminster Hall. An ordinary prison and an ordinary courtroom would be the tiring house and the stage for (ideally) their penultimate performance. Tyburn tree, with hanging, drawing, and quartering were to be the final act: the most humiliating and awful public death that could be staged.

The punishment for high treason will resonate throughout this book, which will take its reader through events between 1660 and 1662, focusing in particular on the experiences of Henry Marten, about whose life before and during the trial and the two subsequent hearings we know a great deal. He it was who, characteristically, while on trial for his life, had managed to slip in that clever little reference to the 'Representative Body of *England*' being responsible for bringing back the king. He had been a House of Commons man since 1640, in spite of his anger with it at times (and his expulsion from it), and even at such a moment could not resist pointing out where his deepest sympathies lay and insisting on the significance of parliament as still the only representative body in the country.

He remains little discussed and perhaps most frequently encountered by modern readers in Aphra Behn's *Oroonoko*, as '*Harry Martin* the great *Oliverian*'.[26] This is a dreadful irony, because Marten – for all his admiration of Cromwell's achievements in the Civil War – hated Cromwell's rise to the king-like power of Lord Protector. In spite of his numerous writings, too, he appears (unindexed) just once in the massive *Oxford Handbook of Literature and the English Revolution*,[27] neither as politician nor as writer. He is, in fact, still not taken very seriously, his louche reputation always tending to dominate references to him and accounts of his life. Charles I was supposed to have dismissed him as '*that whore master*' when they were both in Hyde Park to see the horse racing in the late 1630s, and as having wanted him '*gonne out of the Parke ... or els I will not see the sport*'[28] (it was still a royal park and Charles could insist). But Marten was nevertheless one of the most remarkable, talented, and expressive men to have lived through a quite extraordinary time.

1

Marten

Although Marten is one of the regicides about whom we know most, yet – given his background and his career – he remains not only one of the least understood but one of the oddest. His political activities and significance have over and over again been seen as subsidiary to the unsavoury reputation Charles I was referring to. In December 1648, for example, he walked into the House of Commons side by side with Cromwell after the 'purge' of parliament which they had engineered had rendered it an instrument that could be used to enforce judgement on the king: Marten was one of the most important people in the country. But that same year he had become the target of extraordinary ridicule in royalist newsbooks and pamphlets for his relations with prostitutes. He was presented as a man who, had he 'receyved the 30 pieces of silver' (the Judas money), 'would have gone with it straight to a Bawdy house, and have had a gallant young Wench for it'. He was also described as one who hoped to gain 'the Kingdomes money' (state subsidy) to erect a brothel 'in the City of London', while the reluctance he and the rest of the House of Commons had shown to settle the army's arrears was put down to the way he 'and all the Whoremasters of the House' feared they might then no longer be able to 'keepe halfe a dozen Whores'.[1] And in June 1649 *The Man in the Moon* newsbook offered a fantasy of Marten having 'so over-ridden himself' between one Friday and the Sunday following 'that 'tis

generally thought he will never be serviceable to the state again'.
On the Friday

> he took up two wagg tayles in the Strand, Carried them to
> a leaping-school at Charinge-Crosse, ... where after he had
> feasted them with anchovies, lobsters and caviar and bottles
> of Stipony, he for some weighty reasons adjourned into a
> withdrawing Chamber where all three sat in a close Commit-
> tee from Friday to Sunday noon.[2]

Such sexual exaggerations – of a kind also applied to Cromwell, Peters ('fast and loose carnall prophet and *Arch Jesuited
Incendiary*'[3]), and Thomas Scot but never with such an extraordinary stress on the use of prostitutes – can only be understood
as political propaganda. They tell us where his enemies thought
him vulnerable. But they nevertheless established a default position for commentary on Marten. It was not perhaps so very odd
that in 1724 Bishop Gilbert Burnet in his *History of My Own
Time* should have referred to Marten as 'both an impious and
vicious man [who] delivered himself up unto vice and blasphemy'
or that in 1798 the Reverend Mark Noble should have called
Marten 'licentious, debauched, abandoned' and declared him
'universally scorned'.[4] It is nevertheless surprising that modern
scholarly commentators have taken such propaganda seriously
when commenting on 'Marten's licentious behaviour' or taking
for granted his 'philandering', not to mention his 'hypervirility'.[5]

The reason for Marten's reputation may well come down to
two single facts. After separating from his wife he had for years
enjoyed the love and attention of a much younger mistress, Mary
Ward, to whom he was not (and could not be) married. John
Aubrey (and doubtless others) could therefore declare him a 'For-
nicator', even if an 'honest ingeniose [intelligent]' one. Aubrey
also called him 'a great lover of pretty girls, to whom he was so

liberall that he spent the greatest part of his estate' (he certainly lost a vast amount of money in the middle of his life), although the modern expert who knows most about Marten judges that 'there is little evidence of Marten's womanizing'.[6] There is, however, a report of him together with Mary Ward (sometimes Mary Marten) early in 1653, when they attended a masque given by the Spanish ambassador Alphonso de Cardenas; it was then regarded as scandalous not only that the ambassador should have awarded 'the chief place and respect to Col. H. Martin's mistress', but that she should also have appeared 'finer and more bejewelled than any'.[7] A combination of shock, envy, and scandal thus added to Marten's reputation. But the following year we find him writing to Mary Ward care of her sister Frances Ward 'at the Thatched House in the Rules, Southwark'. In that letter he tenderly calls the one-time bejewelled Mary Ward 'my dear', 'my love', and 'my heart',[8] but – to be living where they did – the Ward family must have had serious financial problems. A house 'in the Rules' – the area around the King's Bench Prison (during the Commonwealth known as the Upper Bench) – was one to which those convicted of criminal debt were confined. In 1653, following his exit from power in the Commonwealth and from his parliamentary privilege of freedom from arrest, Marten would find himself confronted by his creditors – and would thereafter get to know the area very well (a 1660 pamphlet would enquire 'Whether *Harry Martin* loves the Kings Bench Rules better than *Aretines* Postures?'[9] – 'Aretine' being shorthand for the illustrations of sexual positions accompanying Pietro Aretino's sonnets).

Nothing really changed in Marten's sexual reputation over the following period of the Commonwealth. In a pamphlet pre-dating the Restoration by a couple of months '*Henry Martin* Esq.' was declared '*Custos Rotten Whorum* for the suburbs of *London*', while in another publication 'Mal. Marten' appeared in the list of *Common Whores*, and 'Harry Martin' was again included in a list of pimps.[10] He was assumed to be not just a user of brothels ('whoremonger') but an owner and proprietor ('whoremaster'). The lascivious make-believe-almanac *Montelion* of 1660 listed the number of years since special, significant, events had taken place: '*Since H. M. lay with the Beggar Wench* 20', which suggested (although probably exaggerated) the length of time his relationship with Mary Ward had been public knowledge.[11] He was again presented as a pimp: 'The Pope hearing of the beauty of H.M.'s *Lasses*, sends him a letter intreating him to furnish him with one of his best.' A pamphlet which must have been published in London shortly after Marten and others had been committed to the Tower of London at the end of August 1660 showed how Marten could then be seen:

> we shall begin with that ignoble Schismatick,[12] deboist [debauched] Lunatick, and disloyall Subject Henry Martin, whose notorious fame hath been sufficiently spread over all Sodom and Gomorrah, and has the character of courage and abilities, fitting to sit with Betty Blunt, or amongst the greatest kennel of Whores in Crosse-lane or Bloomsbury.[13]

(Cross Lane was at the time notorious.) Another 1660 broadsheet referred to '*Harry Martins Whore*, that was neither *Sound* nor *Pretty*',[14] and, finally, a gathering together in 1662 of old royalist propaganda ballads (*Rump, or, An Exact Collection of the Choycest Poems and Songs Relating to the Late Times*) offered its sadness that Marten was so rotten with the pox that there would not be much point in stringing him up as a regicide: 'he hath been addle [putrid] so many years, / That I fear he will hardly hang together'.[15]

※

If we track back thirty-five years to 1627 we find Marten, a man of twenty-five, making an extremely advantageous marriage to Elizabeth, the eldest daughter of Richard, 1st Lord Lovelace; Marten did not come from an aristocratic family, but his father, the Admiralty judge Sir Henry Marten, had made a fortune, and Marten was his eldest son.

After the birth of four daughters to Marten, Elizabeth had died; the fact that she had died the year the youngest surviving daughter ('Mall') was born suggests that she died in childbirth. What should a man do with four daughters but no wife? Marry again. Marten's second marriage had come in April 1635, to a rich widow of thirty-one, Margaret Staunton, with her own daughter from her first marriage, again a very advantageous arrangement. And with her over the next five years he had four more children – three daughters and at last (he must have thought) a son and heir. But some time subsequent to 1640, at around the time his political career was starting, he and Margaret ceased to live together. She seems to have settled down with at least three of her daughters at Longworth Lodge on one of the Marten estates in Berkshire, while Marten based himself in London. (In September 1652, for example, he was living in Derby House in Channel Row – later Canon Row – just around the corner from the Houses of Parliament.) Aubrey noted that while Marten was living in London,

> When he had found out a ~~pretty wench~~ maried woman that he liked, and he had his Emissaries, male and female to looke out he would contrive such or such a good bargain 20 or 30[li.] per annum land or rent, to have her neer him.[16]

But only 'neer him'. There were no sexual assaults (indeed,

Marten was not the hypervirile sexual predator his enemies – and some modern academics – assume he was). By the 1660s he could refer to Margaret in passing as 'the old one' (L 44) and 'The old woman at Longworth' (L 78), while his relationship with Mary Ward seems to have become a permanent one, in the course of which they had three daughters. Marten's names for the new brood – officially Margaret, Sarah, and Henryetta, but normally Peggie, Moppet (or Poppet), and Bacon-hog – constantly surface in his surviving letters. Henryetta – a feminine version of Henry – celebrated a name that had only arrived in Britain in 1625 with the marriage of the future Charles I to the Roman Catholic Bourbon princess Henriette Marie, thereafter known as Henrietta, whose final child, born June 1644, would also be called Henrietta. It is an odd name for an anti-royalist like Marten to have adopted and should probably be regarded with a wry smile as her parents' ironic gesture towards loyalism and royalism in an increasingly difficult era (it was a name which, to judge by his letters, Marten was very ready to replace with Bacon-hog). The Queen Mother, as Henrietta Maria was named from 1660 onwards, was actually in England from October 1660 until 1661, adding pressure for the regicides' execution (one MP wrote to a friend in November that 'I hear that the Queen Mother sent her secretary to the Houses [of Parliament] to demand justice upon all those that had been the late King's judges'[17]). It was just as well she probably did not know that in 1643 Marten had argued for her impeachment.

By 1640, Marten had – like his father – become a Member of Parliament, the natural role for a comfortably-off country gentleman (he would be even more comfortably-off after his father died in 1641). A good deal in his background would seem to have destined him to be one of those wealthy conservative landowners and MPs who in 1642 might briefly have wondered on which side they belonged in parliament's dispute with the king before equally quickly discovering themselves royalists. Marten's MP brother-in-law Sir George Stonhouse, for example, who had married another of the Lovelace daughters, Margaret, was a convinced royalist, and because of that would be expelled from parliament in 1644; another brother-in-law, John, 2nd Lord Lovelace, who became the heir to the family fortune, was not only a passionate royalist but would be imprisoned in the Tower during the interregnum and fined over £18,000, while the Lovelace family mansion, Ladye Place in Hurley, Berkshire, would be sacked by Parliamentarian soldiers in 1642.

When Marten, however, born to wealth and comfortable ownership, finally at the age of thirty-eight immersed himself in politics as an MP (taking over from his father as a representative for Berkshire) he found himself in a parliament which, between April and August 1641, was responsible for 'Most of the lasting achievements of the English Revolution'.[18] He was on his first committee in December 1640, and a year later was one of the twelve-man committee (along with MPs as distinguished as Pym and John Hampden) arguing for the necessary primacy of the House of Commons over the House of Lords, 'this House being the Representative Body of the whole Kingdom, and their Lordships being but as particular Persons'. The Lords had been obstructive: Marten's committee actually sent out a warning that if the Lords would not collaborate with the Commons in matters 'necessary to the Preservation and Safety of the Kingdom' then the Commons would work 'together with such of the Lords, that are more sensible of the Safety of the Kingdom' – and ignore the rest of the upper chamber.[19] That was revolutionary in 1641; such a promise, to ignore one of the three arms of government (Commons, Lords, king), would have outraged Marten's father.

In the House of Commons, too, Marten had found a place to feel thoroughly at home. It had become clear that his native quick-wittedness, combined with a considerable talent for expressive language, made him not just a successful speaker in the Commons but an excellent man on committees (it has been calculated that he had served on eighty of them before the end of 1641 and on 150 during 1642). 'His Speeches in the house were not long' wrote Aubrey, but 'wondrous poynant' [penetrating] and 'pertinent'. 'He ... alone has sometimes turned the whole house.'[20] And all kinds of new and radical experiences came his way. In January 1642, for example, the king attempted, with an armed force of four hundred, to arrest five members of the House of Commons, including Pym. That was a turning point for many MPs in helping them define what opposition to the king would mean and how necessary it might be. By March 1642 the Commons was using the device of the Ordinance (a decision without the authority of an Act of Parliament but with the effective power of a Law) to enact legislation without the consent of the king, as it struggled into a standpoint of open opposition to him. By August 1642 it had been reported back to Charles that

> it hath been publikely said by Maister *Martin, That Our Office is forfeitable, and that the happinesse of this Kingdom, doth not depend upon Us, or any of the Regall Branches of that Stock* ...

... meaning that neither the king nor his descendants need play any part in the country's future: king and Lords could both be circumvented. Not surprisingly, Charles named '*M. Martin*' as one of the ten Members of Parliament with whom he felt most angry (Pym and Ludlow were among the others) and whom he excepted from the 'Free and General Pardon' he was offering to the rest of those opposed to him.[21]

It is natural that many of Aubrey's surviving anecdotes about Marten should relate to his years in London between 1640 and 1660, and especially to his times in parliament 1640–3, 1646–53, and 1659–60.[22] Aubrey's anecdotes are generally less derogatory than those of the antiquary Anthony Wood, on whose behalf he often made enquiries, and the best of his Parliamentary stories were never taken up by Wood:

> Making an Invective speech one time against old Sir Henry Vane, when he had don with him said – *but for young Sir H. Vane* – and so sate him downe. Severall cryed out. what have you to say to young Sir Harry? he rises up. *why if young Sir H. Vane lives to be old, he will be old Sir Harry.* and so sate downe; and sate the House a laughing, as he oftentimes did.[23]
>
> A Godly member made a motion to have all profane and unsanctified persons expelled the House: H.M. stood up, and moved that all *the Fooles might be putt*-out likewise, and then there would be a thin house.[24]
>
> He was wont to sleep much in the House (at least dog-sleepe[25]) Alderman Atkins made a motion, that such scandalous members as slept, and minded not the businesse of the House should be putt-out. H. M. starts up Mr Speaker! a motion has been to turne out the <u>Noddors</u>, I desire the <u>Noddees</u> may also be turn'd out.[26]

Although these anecdotes about Marten are necessarily unreliable, they are at least consistent with the evidence we have of his behaviour throughout his life and suggest both his resolute independence and his spontaneous wit.

By July 1643 Marten, now one of the leaders of the pro-war party in the Commons, could be found arguing for 'a general and unanimous rising of the people both in this Citie [London], and in other parts of the Kingdome', thus also serving to 'take downe the partition wall betwixt the well-affected, and ill-affected'.[27] At some point he had become a spokesperson for and representative of those outside ordinary representation (not only voters but even those serving on juries had to be owners of freehold property); this provoked complaints that he was putting himself 'at the head of the skumme of the people'.[28] He also worked to do what he could for those who found themselves (often through no fault of their own) incarcerated in debtors' prisons with no prospect of getting out. As – again – Aubrey put it, he was 'a great cultor of Justice, and did alweys in the House take the part of the oppressed'.[29]

※

Some radical thinking, as usual with Marten, lay behind this. A significant strand in his political philosophy – and, in fact, perhaps the driving principle behind everything – was the fact that, years before the idea became widely acceptable, Marten had decided he believed in a republic. Edward Hyde (later Earl of Clarendon, lord chancellor and historian) would recall his own astonishment when, meeting Marten in the churchyard of St Margaret's, Westminster in 1641, and being criticised by Marten for his adherence to those Parliamentarians supporting king and court, he, in turn, pressed Marten to say what *he* thought of the senior MPs (like Pym) 'who governed the house', not believing that Marten could be of their 'opinion or nature'. Marten was honest with him, and

> very frankly answered, that He thought them knaves; and that when they had done as much as they intended to do, they should be used as they had used others.

So what was Marten really in favour of? Hyde was amazed that 'after a little Pause, He very roundly answered, *I do not think one Man wise enough to govern us all*'. This Hyde remembered as 'the first Word He had ever heard any Man speak to that Purpose'.[30]

Such a conclusion may sound unlikely, given that knowledge of the republics in Greek and Roman history would have been an inevitable part of the education of all middle- and upper-class men. But what Hyde meant is that he had never heard anyone actually declare himself in favour of turning England and Ireland into a republic. It is interesting that Marten took a moment before answering, which he does not seem to have done when 'frankly' declaring the senior MPs 'knaves'; what he was going to say was much more dangerous, and he had to consider whether Hyde was the right person to say it to. But when he did say it, he said it 'roundly', that is, bluntly.

Hyde admitted thinking that the idea was such as would only have 'entered into the Hearts of some desperate Persons'. 'Desperate' is a significant word: it means people who have 'lost or abandoned hope; in despair, despairing, hopeless'. And Hyde was the more surprised to hear it because Marten was a 'Gentleman being at that Time possessed of a very great Fortune, and having great Credit in his Country'. He was not on the streets as a beggar, he was not savagely jealous of his social superiors – for those were the only kinds of people whom Hyde imagined could have been opposed to the idea of a king or who might have wished to see Charles removed. Marten's conclusions about how society should be governed were utterly alien to Hyde, who believed that in 1641 the idea of a republic 'would without Doubt, if it had been then communicated or attempted, been the most abhorred by the whole Nation, of any Design that could be mentioned'; and as late as 1648 Hyde would remain baffled that people 'who have good fortunes and excellent understandings' could ever desire such a thing. Surely it was against their own best interests?[31] Marten really was out on a limb.

But from the start of the Civil War in 1642 Marten was perfectly prepared to voice such sentiments. In 1643, for example, in the House of Commons he had offered his support for the

anti-monarchical arguments of the controversial preacher
John Saltmarsh, remarking that he knew of 'no cause why the
destruction of any one family should be put in the ballance
with the destruction of the whole Kingdom'; and then, when
he was pressed to explain what he meant by *'one Family'*, said
it straight out: *'the King and his Children'*.[32] Saltmarsh had
begun to backtrack about the wisdom of getting rid of the royal
family, but Marten was unhesitant, and for that, on 16 August
1643 found himself committed to the Tower of London for two
weeks for high treason and expelled from parliament for three
years, 'his whole life being ript up' (that is, exposed to his disadvantage, according to a triumphant royalist newsbook). He
had indeed been extremely awkward to Puritans like John Pym,
who, according to the report in the same newsbook, took his
chance of attacking Marten, 'falling fowle upon him in a long
Speech, saying, he was a man extreamly guilty of *injustice* and
lewdnesse'. The claimed 'lewdness' may, in fact, have been no
more than another example of the constant propaganda of such
newsbooks against Parliamentarians, as in their attack on Pym
in the next sentence – 'who for *cheating* and *sensuality* may
freely challenge either *man* or *beast'*.[33] Another royalist publication professed itself simply sad that Marten was not being
hanged 'for such faults as highest Treason'.[34]

His loyalties – now outside the House of Commons – had gone in
three main directions. One was for the establishment of a republic. Another would in effect eventually make him a spokesman
for one of the most radical factions in the country. Although he
was not a democrat in the sense that he wanted universal suf-
frage, he was an intensely practical social reformist, insisting, for
example, to a jury, when 'upon the Bench at *Redding'* as a Justice

of the Peace, that they not defer to anyone 'but to put on their hats, as became them, and not to under-value their Countrey, which virtually they were, or words to this effect'.[35] In the second half of the 1640s he grew close to the leadership of the group which came to be called the Levellers, and he was responsible (as the Leveller leader John Lilburne acknowledged) for some of the writing in their great production of 1647–9, a new edition of their old pamphlet *The Agreement of the People*, which became a draft constitution for the Commonwealth; Marten (by then back in parliament) was the only MP who contributed to it. By the late 1640s, however, such a grouping was viewed as far too radical by Parliamentarians like Ireton and Cromwell and was directly opposed by them.

But by then Marten had proved himself a fierce defender of his third loyalty, the power and independence of the very House of Commons which had chosen to expel him – the Commons being the only true representative of the people of England. He also stood out as one who above all believed in the fairer system of representation implicit in the idea of 'a popular election'. The king had endeavoured, throughout the first part of his reign, to rule without taking more notice of parliament than he had needed to. The crucial point of division had, necessarily, been the problem of raising money. Money-raising needed laws. If parliament refused to provide the money, what could or should a king do who still believed that he ruled in the place of God and to whom many thousands of people were loyal simply because he was king?

The king's struggle with parliament had begun in the 1630s and had gone on beyond the start of armed conflict in 1642. London had remained in general Parliamentarian; the king had based himself at Oxford. Eventually, after crucial military defeats, Charles had thrown in his lot with the Scots, traditional enemies of England; in the end, however, they had abandoned him, leaving him for the English Army to confine under house arrest with no intention at that time of bringing him to trial. But their experience of him had involved a good deal of double-dealing, as Charles twisted and turned, trying to retain what power and influence he could.

✳

Marten had actually exited the House of Commons again in May or June 1648, angry that negotiations with the king (against which he had warned in his pamphlet of a few months earlier, *The Parliaments Proceedings Justified, in Declining a Personall Treaty with the King*) seemed accepted as the way forward and convinced that at that date he could be of more practical than parliamentary assistance; he reckoned the House would 'rather bee served than waited on'.[36] Earlier on, when the Commons had given Marten the right to seize the property of anyone at war with parliament, the House of Lords had been scandalised when he removed two of the king's horses from the Royal Mews. He had justified himself by pointing out that he had been 'given authority to take "the King's Ship, and Forts, for the Defence of the Kingdom, and might as well take his Horses"', but the Lords insisted on his 'disrespect to their Lordships'.[37] In 1648 he raised his own troop of cavalry: 'by the *help of some friends & my own care* & cost I have gotten up a troop of honest men ... resonably well appointed, notwithstanding the strange obstructions I mett with from those that owed their contrey as much assistance as my self'.[38] This was to be 'an armed band ... pledged to fight against anyone, royalist, Scot or Parliamentarian, who might seek to put the King back on his throne';[39] as if to prove this, just three days after the execution of the king – so the moment that danger was past – 'the Horse, under the Command of Colonel Martyn' would be incorporated in the main army.

Illustration 5: 'Said to be of Henry Marten': oil painting

Illustration 3 (see page xxi) – especially when set alongside the 1650 portrait of Cromwell – offers no evidence of the military capacities of a man so often referred to by his contemporaries as Colonel Marten. Illustration 5, however, 'Said to be of Henry Marten', shows a soldier; it is a portrait that also deserves to be set beside a Cromwell portrait, one dating from around 1649 by Robert Walker. It could probably not have been painted without the artist having some kind of access to Walker's Cromwell portrait (perhaps via an engraving), which must date it to some time in 1649 or later, although it is hard to reconcile the man it shows with the apparently much older eminence in the Lely portrait (Marten was forty-seven years old in 1649).[40]

※

By the end of 1648 Marten was one of a number of MPs and senior army figures who had concluded that all the sacrifices of the Civil War must not be given up in some kind of agreement with the king jumbled together by a still traditionally inclined parliament (which was what seemed most likely). From Marten's point of view, the army's 'purge' of parliament on 6 December 1648 was the only way to break the logjam: the number of sitting MPs had been reduced from 490 to a maximum of 250 members, with far fewer MPs, something around sixty-five, actually attending as the Rump. Marten's riotously unfair pamphlet, *A Word to Mr Wil. Prynn Esq. and Two for the Parliament and Army*, coming out right at the start of 1649, showed him ridiculing the influential MP William Prynne as well as '*Reproving*' the unpurged parliament; he declared himself prepared to

> honour Parliaments so long as they Act in Order to the publique good: But if, like standing pooles, they only gather mudd and filth, I think it very fit to cleanse them.[41]

Marten also made clear his belief that the only way forward would be a future government operating without the king. Kings were simply not to be trusted. He offered the example of Richard II, who – having apparently submitted to reforms instigated by his

Illustration 6: Oliver Cromwell: oil painting by Robert Walker, *c.* 1649

uncle the Duke of Gloucester, the Earl of Arundel, and the Earl
of Warwick – eventually called a parliament, overawed it with
his army, had Gloucester and Arundel killed, and Warwick sent
into exile. Marten concluded 'Better things are not to be expected
from this King', who was 'worse than the worst of his ancestors'.[42]

And, finally – the man of words as ever – after the execution of Charles he would supervise the twenty-seven-page declaration, published on 22 March 1649, which was used as the official explanation of what parliament had done in executing the king, abolishing the House of Lords and governing via parliament and a Council of State: *A Declaration of the Parliament of England, Expressing the Grounds of Their Late Proceedings, and of Setling the Present Government in the Way of a Free State*. This document was not only published in English but versions in Latin (*Parliamenti Anglia Declaratio*), French, and Dutch were also produced for the edification of those in other countries: it set out exactly what it hoped had happened:

> The *Representatives* of the *People* now Assembled in *Parliament*, have judged it *necessary* to change the *Government* of this *Nation* from the former *Monarchy*, (unto which by many injurious incroachments it had arrived) into a *Republique*, and not to have any more a *King* to *tyrannize* over them.[43]

As his father's heir Marten had spent a vast amount of inherited and borrowed money on the Parliamentary military campaigns between 1642 and 1648 (described on 3 July 1649 as 'several great Sums of Money disbursed by Colonel *Henry Marten*, for the Service of the Parliament'); a consequence of his loyalty to the Parliamentarian campaign had, for example, been that one of his own properties, Beckett House near Shrivenham, had been badly damaged by royalist soldiers. In July 1649 the Commons took account of this and also of other 'great Losses sustained by him' in its decision to recompense him with land taken from defeated aristocrats, so that he ended up with estates in Shropshire, around Leominster, and near Hartington, on the

Derbyshire-Staffordshire border, as well as at Eyensham, near the old Marten estates in Berkshire. Still later he was repaid a lump sum of £3,600, as 'money formerly lent and long since payable'.

The estates were, in fact, extremely difficult to manage. But what we know about Marten's relations with the stewards who ran them[44] suggests that he also had no head for business (and little talent in choosing either the right managers or the proper people to whom he decided to sell property); the new land always appeared to bring in more debts and trouble than profit. As we might expect from a man of his political beliefs, too, he was more concerned with fairness and traditional rights than a successful landowner at that period would have been. He was opposed to enclosing his land, for example, whereas the farm next to his in Berkshire did exactly that,[45] and there is evidence of his being a generous and forgiving landowner and landlord, even when he was losing money and authority in his new possessions. Aubrey believed him 'not at all covetous'.[46]

※

By the early 1650s Marten could also see with horror what was happening to the infant republic he had helped bring into existence. There was probably more savagery than good humour in a remark Aubrey says he made in the Commons, some time between 1649 and 1653:

> Oliver Cromwell once in the House, called him jestingly, or scoffingly Sir Harry Martin. H. M. rises, and bowes, I thanke your Majestie, *I alwayes thought when you were King that I should be knighted.*[47]

Frighteningly apposite and prescient: Marten saw, well before it came, Cromwell's rise to king-like power, when he would no longer need the Commons. In 1660, too, while on trial, Marten would offer a startling image of what on reflection he had concluded about the rise of 'our first false General':

> Had *I* suspected that the Axe which took off the late Kings head, should have been made a stirrop for our first false General, *I* should sooner have consented to my owne death then his. (*L* 3)

For Marten the turning point had finally come with Cromwell's expulsion of the sitting parliament, using military force, on 20 April 1653. It was not a fully representative parliament at that point, following its 'purge' in December 1648, but it was still an elected parliament. After Cromwell had closed it down it was first replaced by a thirteen-man Council of State[48] and then, in the summer of 1653, by the short-lived assembly which became known as the 'Barebones Parliament'.

Marten wrote to Cromwell in the summer of 1653, apparently about an invitation that he serve in one of the new bodies, probably the parliament, '*declining, in very plain terms, to have anything to do with it*'. 'I cannot apprehend my selfe either call'd or qualified sufficiently for such a trust', he remarked, and then he went on the attack. Cromwell, it was famously remarked in 1657, 'is naturally cholerick, and must call Men Rogues, and go to cuffs [i.e. throw punches]', and Marten made a note of one of Cromwell's violent assertions on the morning of the April expulsion: 'the people shall not have their liberty, I say the people shall not have their liberty'.[49] That struck directly at everything Marten had been trying to ensure, for Cromwell had done something which neither James I nor Charles I had ever dared to do, not just suspend or prorogue parliament or attack individual members but expel the whole body, with military force, that April morning: 'the same thing which the last King and his Father did so long designe, and attempt, your Ex^{cy} hath brought about'.

Marten also attacked Cromwell for prioritising army over parliament and insisted that the army had been an insatiable devourer of the country's resources – and one that had not even been grateful to the people who had been 'so eminent benefactors' to it and who had sacrificed so much on its behalf:

> nothing is more frequent in the mouthes even of the meaner sort of People then ye ingratitude of the Army towards those who not only raised them ...[50]

Marten, in turn, had been savagely and publicly assailed by Cromwell as a 'whoremonger' (Charles I had preferred 'whoremaster'[51]) during the latter's denunciation of parliament before he drove the members out. But from that point onwards, no longer an MP, not only was Marten no longer near the centre of power: he could see that the country had lost its chance of ever being a republic. The Lord General of the army was the only remaining real authority in the country, and on 26 December 1653 Cromwell assumed the title of Lord Protector.

※

That winter Marten drafted a Latin panegyric to Cromwell. What survives is an unfinished fair copy, heavily corrected; it must have been written around the time that Cromwell assumed the title of Lord Protector, and it is at times genuine panegyric: Cromwell's military prowess is magnificent, he has 'a hand invincible in war, and greater in response to dangers, the force of his spirit enduring the struggles of summer and winter campaigns'. And yet even such admiration is tempered in the final words of the line: Cromwell's prowess has been 'experienced in advancing on enemies or repressing citizens'. The word translated as 'repressing', *compescere*, 'could be used relatively benignly to refer to pruning plants, but the basic association was of chains'.[52] And lines such as 'This famous Cromwell fills the throne to the acclamation of the British people' show the double-sidedness of the poem: it *is* a throne that Cromwell has filled, he has made himself a monarch, and the British people were never for a moment consulted. A couple of lines later the poem refers snarlingly to the way Cromwell 'did not court the votes of the fickle people' – that is, the votes of people whom he, Cromwell, despises because he thinks them fickle and to whom his only response could be 'the people shall not have their liberty'. A Parliamentarian and believer in elections such as Marten would never have been so rude about the electorate.

Towards the end of the poem, too, a series of questions undermines the ideas of achievement and stability that the poem had been inculcating: 'Where do his achievements come from? What a great man he is! where will he go in the end? where is it right for him to stop?'[53] Marten's is not a great work of irony and admiration like Andrew Marvell's 'Horatian Ode', but it was characteristic of him (although using a language other than English) to have described the awful limitations of one-man rule. It should remind us of his remark back in 1641: *'I do not think one Man wise enough to govern us all.'*

※

In 1653, too, within months of losing his position as an MP, for a complicated muddle of reasons – 'lavishly supporting the radical war effort, high living, the cost of supporting his family, investing in his brother's ambitions to be a Caribbean planter, and having been awarded lands which proved both underproductive and heavily encumbered'[54] – Marten was in real financial trouble; one friend commiserated with him over the fact that he had been arrested for debt, owing as he did £29,000.[55] That is a terrifying amount, and it is not surprising that he never recovered. At the start of 1655, for example, he would be convicted of 'outlawry', a punishment for contempt of court in not appearing to answer an indictment or defend a personal action or for disobedience to a judgement of the court. Outlawry for debt was frequent; the outlawed person was incapacitated from prosecuting an action for his own benefit, although he could still defend himself. Marten was, however, still engaged in various commercial trans-actions which a constantly reinvented (but still unrepresentative) House of Commons would query. For instance, in March 1658 the Customs and Excise Committee would demand that he pay the £20 'for one tun of French wine', which he had bought off the committee as prize goods, payment for it being long overdue. His taste for the good life continued undiminished in spite of his lack of money. He would, in fact, be committed to prison for debt in 1655 and 1656 and was in the Upper Bench Prison in 1659, when parliament – in the process of reassembling its old Rump House of Commons from 1648–53 – had to list him as 'Martin, Henry, a prisoner in execution' (indicating that the 'person of a debtor' had been imprisoned 'in default of payment'). Parliamentary immunity as an MP would then have kept him out of prison and out of the hands of his creditors.

It must be to this period that an anecdote belongs concerning General Monck, widely (and rightly) then believed to be plan-ning to help Charles II back on to the throne. Monck's chaplain later recalled how Monck was 'set upon in Jest by a late *Long-Parliament-Common-wealths-man*, who was good at it'. This was Marten, who had asked Monck whether his real aim was a king or a commonwealth? Monck insisted that he had always been in favour of a commonwealth, upon which Marten told him the story of a city tailor found out in the country carry-ing a pick-axe and spade. Asked what he was doing, the tailor replied that he was going to measure a man for a new suit of clothes: 'these are the Measures now in fashion'. Marten left it to Monck to see the point of the story: that for a man intend-ing to maintain a commonwealth, Monck's New Model Army was an utterly inappropriate tool, although it was the one 'now in fashion'. With 'pick-axe and spade' indeed, Monck looked more like a man intending to bury the Commonwealth than one hoping to preserve it.[56]

And – all thoughts of Commonwealth forgotten – that is what Monck did with his mission to collect Charles in May 1660 and place him on the throne.

2

Tower

In preparation for their trial at the Old Bailey in the autumn of 1660, a group of respectable middle-aged and elderly men – many of them not only belonging to the nation's governing class but the actual makers of its policy – had been locked up without any legal preliminaries, first in the less-than-tender hands of the Serjeant at Arms of the House of Commons, James Northfolke, then (towards the end of August) in the Tower of London. This was where those accused of high treason were always imprisoned (famous figures out of English history such as Thomas More, Thomas Cromwell, and Walter Raleigh had all been confined to the Tower before trial and execution). Like most of the events of 1660 these imprisonings happened quickly and without a shot being fired and represented just a fraction of the enormous change ensuing on the Restoration, as the English establishment recast itself into a new shape with new personalities in charge.

When Marten was brought to the Tower of London on 25 or 27 August 1660, his time in the Upper Bench had ended only a short while before; prison for him – unlike for most of his fellow prisoners – was no new experience. For the oddest of reasons, we know a good deal about his experiences in the Tower from a source that only came into existence because in 1662 the minor poet and impecunious royalist scribbler Edmund Gayton reckoned he could exploit Marten's old reputation as womaniser and his new notoriety as regicide. Gayton put into print an utterly random collection of eighty-nine letters from Marten to Mary Ward written over the previous seven years;[1] Gayton gave his compilation the inflammatory title *Coll: HENRY MARTEN's Familiar LETTERS TO HIS LADY OF DELIGHT* (the title inside slightly altered to *Coll: Henry Martins FAMILIAR EPIS-TLES to His Lady of Pleasure*). It looks like an attempt to make as much money as might still be made out of Marten's scandal-ous reputation, while simultaneously taking him to task for his career as regicide and reprobate.

Gayton added numerous prefaces, interferences, and prelimi-nary letters, including one ending 'Well Sir, you are now in the Tower, keep there, and if you can recant, repent' and advising him to 'Forsake *Mall* [i.e. Mary Ward] ... and all the Witchcrafts of your life'. The most significant addition was the first item of all, not, in fact, a letter to Mary but Marten's lengthy justi-fication of the part he had played in the execution of Charles I, which was probably composed in August or September 1660 when Marten was still expecting – as many others were – to be banished. One MP wrote to an old friend on 14 August that the 'Bill of Indemnity is returned from the House of Lords and will be speedily dispatched'; the House of Commons wanted 'the King's Judges to be banished', although, he confessed, 'that is not yet concluded'.[2] A little earlier in the summer, Marten had informed Mary that '*I* was told yesterday that all we (except two of us, who are in more favour) must be banished' (*L* 67); he could write about 'the hopes of my being banished' (*L* 72) having heard (probably rather later) that his 'Cousin J. Y—' – perhaps John Yate, 2nd Baronet of Buckland – 'believes onely banishment is intended at last' (*L* 33). In his letter justifying himself Marten imagined 'the manifest inconveniencies and dif-ficulties *I* carry with me for the etching [eking] out[3] a pursued life in a strange land'. He would inevitably be 'pursued' if ban-ished because some royalist sympathisers – 'our old enraged and new empowred enemies' (*L* 1) – were never going to give up the hope of achieving what they deemed justice: royalist sympathis- ers had, for example, assassinated Isaac Dorislaus, the Dutch lawyer who had given advice about the legal status of a king before the trial of Charles I, when Dorislaus had briefly returned to the Netherlands.[4] But 'etching out a pursued life' was one trial Marten did not have to confront. He was never given the chance.

Gayton also manufactured or stole or grafted together twelve extra letters purporting to be those to Mary Ward from Mar- ten's 'rival', their servant and messenger Dick Pettingall, and added them at the end, along with a letter denouncing Marten as 'a most desperate villain, and not fit to live in a Kingdom' because of his justification of the execution of Charles I, while also employing the stereotype of Marten as 'an unrepenting Whoremaster' (*L* 91–2). Such additions succeeded in bulking the book up to over 100 pages. Not a single authentic letter in the collection can safely be dated subsequent to December 1661, which suggests that they were in Gayton's hands soon after that.

Some of the letters – nineteen or twenty – were written before Marten arrived in the Tower and some while he was still a free man, before 20 June 1660; another eighteen letters are of uncer- tain date. It is possible that some of the letters written from prison date from previous periods of incarceration (he was in the Upper Bench Prison in 1659, for example), but there are still nearly fifty letters that can be assigned to his time in the Tower. There were at least two printings of the *Familiar Letters* (in Oxford) in 1662 and 1663, and eleven copies of the 1662 edition appear to survive today in libraries, with a similar number from 1663, suggest- ing a fairly widespread sale; a supposed 'Second Edition' sold in London in 1685 (eight copies apparently surviving) would claim that they had been 'Found in his Misses Cabinet' but would omit all of Gayton's impertinent additions.

Gayton can never actually have read what he had stolen. The

letters are remarkable not (as Gayton claimed) because they were 'most of them salacious' but for the picture they paint of a family father very conscious of his partner's 'three arm-loads of treasure' (*L* A2, 77), while constantly breaking out into exclamations of tenderness for her, too: 'rest, my sweet Soul, thy own every day that goes over my head, every night too, whether I talk to thee or no, whether *I* dream of thee or no' (*L* 36).

But the letters also offer useful corrective sidelights to, for example, the famous account of life in the Tower in 1664 in *Memoirs of the Life of Colonel Hutchinson*, put together by John Hutchinson's wife after his death, and describing the same Lord Lieutenant of the Tower, Sir John Robinson, as had been there in Marten's time. Robinson indeed appears fairly often in Marten's letters but nearly always as a problem to be evaded. Samuel Pepys knew Robinson and thought him 'a talking, bragging Bufflehead', dismissing him as someone who had simply jumped the right way in the spring of 1660 when he had managed to help welcome Charles II to London: 'a fellow that would be thought to have led all the City in the great business of bringing in the King ... I am confident there is no man almost in the City that cares a turd for him, nor hath he brains to out-wit any ordinary tradesman'.[5] Given his reputation for 'bringing in the King' – something which got him his baronetcy and his job as Lord Lieutenant of the Tower – it was not surprising that Robinson was especially hostile towards the regicides he had in his prison. He was, incidentally, paid £200 a year as Lord Lieutenant of the Tower, but everyday responsibility devolved on to the gentleman porter. At the start of 1660 this had been John Baldwin, paid £22 14s. 8d. a year, but it became clear over the next six months that the post (along with a host of other well-remunerated positions) would go to someone else. Various people petitioned for it, but eventually in July 1660 it was awarded to Major Alvarny Pinckney, a royalist war hero. The gentleman porter also had various

ways of making money: he it was, for example, who regulated
– and earned rent from – the 'tenements and shops' scattered all
over the so-called Liberty of the Tower, inside the castle itself,
and also in the streets nearby. Under him were the whole person-
nel of the Tower; there was also a yeoman porter specifically in
charge of the warders, in theory forty of them, although Robinson 'had not near so many, but filled up the list with false names,
and took the pay to himself'.[6] Or so Hutchinson alleged.

Hutchinson fought a series of running verbal battles with
Robinson and was also notably stand-offish with one of the
warders who offered to help him; Marten was charming, especially to Robinson's subordinates – in particular to the second
in command, the gentleman porter, and to the various keepers
and warders with whom he came in contact, and with care he
managed to do and get almost exactly what he wanted.

So, for example, what kind of access to fresh air might be
allowed to such prisoners? Hutchinson, his wife complained,
was 'kept close prisoner, and had no air allowed him, but a pair
of leads over his chamber, which were so high and cold he had
no benefit by them',[7] 'leads' being the flat lead roof. Hutchinson
was there in winter, so it was not surprising that he didn't get
out much. Marten, though, was happy to tell Mary that '*I shall
have a time to trust thee with my neck upon the leads before I
am a week older, I hope*' (L 51); and he also acquired permission
'to walk once a day into the Gentleman Porters lodgings, and on
the top of his leads' (L 35). He had clearly established an excellent relationship with the gentleman porter to be allowed such
privileges; in summer he was actually allowed into 'the Gentleman Porters lodgings', where he 'tickled his Gooseberry-bushes'
(L 44).

And, most important of all, the gentleman porter helped him
manage visits from Mary. There had for years been fairly strict
controls on who might be allowed into the Tower – visitors were

(at least in theory) restricted to those to whom 'leave' had been given: 'None to bee admitted to any prison wthout the privitie [private consent] of the lieuten'nt, or such as hee shall appoint in his absence'.[8] Wives and close family were generally allowed, unless there was a sudden and inexplicable tightening of security, as when Marten complained that 'My son was not suffered to see me yesterday' (L 75). Servants were sometimes allowed (although not normally into the closely guarded areas of the prison, unless they actually lodged there together with their masters). Girlfriends or mistresses required very special conditions to allow them access. Marten had tried getting Mary in as a special favour by requesting permission from Sir John Robinson, although he knew he had to be careful and – for example – not ask for a favour when Sir John's only son was ill – 'till that be over ... there is no coming neer him for any favour'. On another occasion, too, he got a helpful warning from the gentleman porter that 'Sir J. is a little fusty [ill-humoured, peevish] to day; he thinks not fit to be spoken to' – so that asking him for anything would be unwise (L 13, 64). But the gentleman porter also let him know when Sir John was going to be away. Marten's ability to get on with people like the gentleman porter helped him hugely. He also recorded, on occasion, borrowing money from other prisoners when the need arose; he was surrounded by the kind of small support network that was crucial for individuals to survive decently in prison.

And then there was the whole matter of mail and servants' access. In theory, prisoners might neither send nor receive letters that had not been scrutinised by the authorities (they were political prisoners, after all, at a time when the new regime was very worried about committed republicans or Fifth Monarchists staging some kind of uprising and making the regicides focal points of support). But whether a prisoner actually managed to receive letters – or get them out – depended partly on the helpfulness and discretion of warders, keepers, and servants and partly on the prisoners' own ingenuity (even Hutchinson had been 'within an hour of his imprisonment … instructed by another prisoner'[9] on a safe and convenient way of getting letters out of the prison). At times, however, servants – with or without letters – were simply denied access to the Tower. One of Mary's letters only reached Marten because the servant (Robin) who had been sent with it but had been turned away, by chance met Marten's twenty-three-year-old daughter Jane (known often as Jinny) – 'upon whom he stumbled in the street' (L 62), as Marten put it. And she could bring in the letter.

It was Jane, of all his daughters, who was mentioned most often in Marten's surviving letters to Mary Ward. So far as we know she never married, and it looks as if she were the one who spent most time and trouble over him, as is suggested by a letter she wrote three years earlier, apparently at a time when Marten had descended into terrible financial trouble and had been confined to 'his house in the Rules in Southwarke' – exactly as Mary's sister had earlier been:

Sir, The hopes I have had of seing you every day hath made me forbear to trouble you with writing till now. I am very sory to hear you are so incumber'd with fresh troubles before you are rid of the old. I whish with all my heart I knew how I might be so serviceable to you as that I could be capable of doing you any good, for indeed it is a very great trouble to me that ther is none of us is able to doe any more then wish and pray for your happy deliverance out of your troubles, and according to your comands bear it out till it shall pleas God either to make me more serviceable or less burdensome to you. So with my humble duty I rest,

Sir, your most obedient child till death,

Jane Marten.[10]

The reference in the letter to her wish to be 'less burdensome to you' reminds us that Marten was probably responsible for the financial support of his unmarried daughters. But the other telling reference is to Marten's own instruction to everyone to 'bear it out' with him. They simply had to be tough and resilient and wait. If that had been true in 1657, it was even more the case when Marten was in the Tower in 1660 awaiting trial.

※

It is actually very hard to generalise about conditions of life in the Tower. Everything seems to have depended upon: first, what friends the prisoners had outside prison; second, their state of health; third, how they behaved; and fourth, and most important, on what kind of money they had. That made an enormous difference. Appropriate payments to the right people were a simple way of assisting with problems. When Marten had been released from his first experience of the Tower in September 1643, one detail had been revealing: perhaps because he was an MP, he had been discharged without having to pay any fees to his gaoler. That was unusual; paying for one's own imprisonment was the rule. Hutchinson, for example, was faced with a bill for fifty pounds from Robinson for only twenty-four weeks in the Tower, as a result of which he wrote Robinson a long and threatening letter (and got a copy out of the Tower, too) listing the various corrupt practices he had experienced, one being that Robinson 'took the most considerable prisoners ... into his own house, and made them pay excessive rates for bed-rooms', while imposing 'his man, Cresset, over them, making them pay him for attendance'.[11] It was common for an upper-class prisoner to bring a servant into gaol with him, but Robinson was attempting to impose his own servant (and demanding money for the privilege) in his lodgings in what is today called the Queen's House.

The prison – like most prisons of the period – was organised around the individual rooms in which prisoners were locked up at night and common areas where they could socialise: the best (and most expensive) individual rooms were often in the prison governor's own residence. At some point between 1660 and 1662 Marten, too, found himself faced with a bill for 'fees' for his accommodation from Robinson, 'who claims 30 l. due still' (*L* 44). Whether or when he paid it is unknown, but he would not have responded with the kind of threatening letter Hutchinson came up with. If anyone was capable of getting a favour out of Robinson, it was Marten.

※

People in the West today have a lot to learn about prison in the seventeenth century.[12] Not only had lodging to be paid for, so had nearly all food (there was sometimes a daily bread allowance). There might also be fees for leaving. On the other hand, a system that was inherently corrupt (the people running it having every opportunity to exploit the people committed to their charge and constantly doing so) also allowed unexpected freedoms. Money could nearly always buy privileges and opportunities, and Marten's letters to Mary Ward are actually a good example of something which – under a strict prison regime for political prisoners – ought never to have got out of prison at all but which did, because of fees, tips, and charm being distributed in the right places. And the same applies to their opportunities for seeing each other.

One revealing thing in Marten's letters, however, is the lack of reference to religion. He appears to have had little or no real belief in a providential God, although he regularly invoked God's name, the first four surviving letters in the *Familiar Letters* throwing up 'My person being hitherto by Gods providence preserved' (*L* 1), 'My Dear, it is indeed a very great blessing that you have all your healths, as I have mine, *I* thank God' (*L* 6), 'Munday is neer, till then, and afterwards, and for ever, God keep thee, and my soul' (*L* 7), '*I* am very well (I thank God)' (*L* 8). In all eighty-nine letters he mentions God twenty-one times – but always formulaically, never piously. To call him 'a freethinker',[13] though, is to go too far. Anthony Wood reckoned that Marten and his friends were 'of the natural religion',[14] indicating that they thought belief in God obvious, sensible, indeed self-interested, but Marten's own opinion of God was grounded in his belief that 'what ever hath bene said by any yet concerning him is but ... opinion'.

This would have encouraged him in his toleration of Roman Catholics, Jews, Antinomians, and Anabaptists; he was, thought Aubrey, 'as far from a Puritane as light from darknesse',[15] not only 'libertarian' but also 'undogmatic'. Being prescriptive was pointless; he had written how the only way to 'suppresse Blasphemies, Sects, and Heresies' was 'by convincing the Blasphemer, the Sectary and the Heretick' and not by preaching at them.

> When Christ is contented to tolerate the tares among the corn I would not have you call toleration accursed, especially as you may be deceived in discerning tares from corn.[16]

The historian Blair Worden has concluded that

> Among Roundheads Marten's anti-Puritanism was exceptional. So was his disrespect for the doctrine of providence. An alertness to God's presence in the world was an inbuilt feature of most mid-seventeenth-century minds, Cavalier as well as Roundhead.

And Marten never tried to comfort Mary – or himself – with

religious counsel or 'Puritan providentialism'.[17] This is significant, as he had a good deal of comforting to do: for example, at one of the worst moments of their common life, when he had heard how the House of Commons had finally agreed on the long-threatened Act of Parliament which would inevitably lead to his execution. He held back the news for a couple of days but then told her, reckoning that it would be better for her to hear it from him. And he offered not a word of religious comfort.

The contrast with another almost exactly contemporaneous couple of letters from the Tower – those of John Cooke, his fellow regicide – could hardly be greater. One from Cooke to his wife started:

> My Dear Lamb, blessed be God for Jesus Christ, and for a Prison, where I find much of his comforting presence; tell Sister *Jones* that she keeps but two or three Sabbaths in a Week, but in Prison every day is a Christian Sabbath; not onely to cease from sin, but to Praise God, singing *Hosannaes* and *Hallalujahs*. I can but smile to think that they cannot hinder me from Preaching, for I Preach twice every day to my self ...

And indeed Cooke went on preaching to himself for the rest of his letter. It was only at rare moments – such as in his words towards the end, 'Therefore my Dear Sweeting'[18] – that he made any apparent address to the woman to whom he was writing rather than to himself, and even the word 'Sweeting' related to a reference just made to life as a 'bitter-sweeting'; it was not simply an endearment.

But Cooke's letters were in the old tradition of letters as moral and religious epistles; not, in fact, personal but designed to be shared with a circle of people (Sister Jones was probably one of the congregation). Other, more ordinary letters that Cooke may have sent were neither preserved nor printed;

everyday, bread-and-butter, common-or-garden letters, with kisses, endearments, and requests ... the kinds of thing that hardly ever survive but do, in quite an exceptional way, by pure accident, in Marten's letters.

Marten, too, found other ways of offering consolation, in mutton he had tried to send, in bacon ('*Longworth* commodity' probably means that), shillings – and tenderness ('buss' means 'kiss'). A complete letter runs:

> *My Soul,*
>
> When shall *I* see thee? when shall *I* have thee within some compass of being able to send to thee, or hear from thee once every day? The ugly Carriers Porters wife cheated me, when she told me she would come againe, and perhaps cheated thee of thy shoulder of mutton. I have now sent thee a little of my *Longworth* commodity, and a scrapp of the business, *viz.* 4 s. Buss my little brats for,
>> My Heart,
>>> Their
>>>> Daddy, *H.M.* (*L* 18)

※

When committed to the Tower in August 1660 Marten was a man still possessed of an income – something like £100 a year, or £2 a week, via his sister Elizabeth. He owned land (although it would very shortly be repossessed), and land produced rent from his tenants. The way he actually received his income had, however, to become more and more devious, as his estates were gradually appropriated following his imprisonment. Some had already been sold to individuals he knew, like the Berkshire property owner John Loder and Marten's old friend (and fellow political activist) Major John Wildman, probably in the hope that they would therefore not be seized and that he would continue to benefit from them, courtesy of the people who now held them. But there were constant problems, often noted in the letters to Mary, John Loder being at one point unwilling to pay 'what *I* pressed him to', while the authorities – probably rightly – suspected 'that all is juggling betwixt him and me' (*L* 6–7). And in November 1661 John Wildman was arrested and committed to prison, thus bringing to an end any chance of income from *him*. It looks as if Marten, in the end, came to depend entirely on what his sisters and daughters and their husbands could provide for him.

He had done his best to secure Mary Ward's future by making over to her nearly 750 acres of land at Hartington, in Derbyshire, including a property, Fern House, but it is most unlikely that she was ever able to possess it or make use of it, as the Hartington land was returned to its original owner following the Restoration. Marten felt responsible for passing on from his trickle of income what he could to her, in cash when possible. He told her, probably in the summer of 1660, about 'my allowance, wherein thou may'st be sure to have a pretty share' (*L* 72–3). At other times he passed on what he could simply in the form of food; he sent her, for example, 'a piece of Venison, and a Cheese from my sister E—'s, and after cheese nothing (thou know'st) or that which is next to nothing, two poor pieces of silver' (*L* 58): perhaps two silver sixpences. The time had been when, in the summer of 1660, he had been able to send her a gold coin or two – 'the other odde spanker' (*L* 67) – but not any more. The dispatch of food was, nevertheless, an example of how the problems and trials of life as a prisoner in the Tower could, along with visits from loved ones, be managed by the resourceful.

3

Tending and Scribbling

From where, however, does one get joints of meat when one is locked up as a political prisoner in the Tower of London? Letter after letter reveals Marten not only sending out to Mary Ward what he gets from his relations – like the venison and the cheese – but also fresh meat: on three occasions, for example, a 'leg of mutton' (*L* 14, 52, 78), also a 'shoulder of Mutton' (*L* 18, 35), 'a neck of Mutton' (*L* 45). The answer is simple. There is food on sale in the Tower: a 'butcher's man' is sometimes even allowed into Marten's closely guarded quarters (*L* 36, 51). There is also bread baked in the Tower itself, Marten on one occasion sending Mary Ward 'two Tower loaves of two sorts' (*L* 15). And there are two further possibilities for acquiring food. One is giving his messenger the money to buy things on his way to Mary but more common seems the opportunity given by the individual traders who come into the prison in the morning and set up stalls. Prisoners like Marten employ someone to go into the market area of the Tower and buy things, so that he can tell Mary 'Mean while here is a dozen of egs for thee, and a pound of butter, just now bought of a countrey Hegler' (*L* 18); better than 'the piti-full butter' (*L* 36) she had received a day or so earlier, which had probably been from the Tower itself, butter 'such as is brought into the Tower' (*L* 76) being superior. On another occasion he mournfully tells her how late his own warder has been in unlock-ing his room ('it was past nine this morning'), so that by the time he can send anyone 'for any thing the best of the market is gone' (*L* 26). The warder is

> a very civil person to me when he is with me … but he is just the worst Keeper in the Tower for keeping his times, when he is from me, that he makes me so uncertain in sending to thee, whereas all other prisoners are unlocked before 7 in the morning; he makes me stay till 8, 9, 10, and past; it is almost 9 now, yet I am fast. (*L* 76)

Another day Marten is luckier and is able to get 'butter at market for thee while it was to be had' (*L* 61).

In such various ways Marten helps – while in funds, and while she is in London – to keep Mary Ward supplied. It is understood between them that, while he occasionally sends her cash, he will do what he can to send substance, as he tells her in the summer of 1661: 'all my business is to provide relief where I can, and when' (*L* 44). The letters are, in fact, nearly all of them domestic and – if at times philosophical about his position – also extremely practical. They have been criticised by a modern reader for being 'filled with banal housekeeping exchanges',[1] but that underestimates the necessity Marten feels to list what he is sending out, so that Mary can tell what has been dispatched, and this is especially so when he has given his messenger money, 'money to buy thee nine pound of soap, two pound of candles, one of rush, the other of cotton of eights, and a sixpenny loaf' (*L* 22). As a result, at times whole sentences in his letters resemble nothing so much as grocery lists – items mostly of food and drink being sent out to wherever Mary Ward is lodging (sometimes apparently in Marten's own lodgings, at times at her sister's house in Southwark, and also in Kennington). Hence 'Here is a pint bottle of new Canary a Hollingbury Hen, half a score Puddings, and four half-crownes' (*L* 58), and – on a cold day in May – 'bread, and beer, and sparaguss, and 3 s. to buy thee coles' (*L* 26).

It is understandable that he recorded in his letters the items he was sending out: cash in particular needed to be noted. On what must have been a hot summer day, in contrast,

> I am able to give thee a bottle of rare Sack too, so thou canst keep it cool, either in gravell, or in water, with salt-peter in it; any other water will make it hotter; and to give thee a piece of roasting Beef, and a shoulder of Mutton; Veale *I* would have had, but the butcher dares not kill any for feare of the weather. (*L* 35)

And, one Wednesday in 1660 or 1661:

> *My sweet Love,*
> I Cannot think every day too often to send to thee, and hear from thee (at least of thee.) All the token *I* have for thee is an Orange or two, a piece of bread (halfe what it was last) and a piece of butter (half a pound) and just such a weight of Sassages. (*L* 50)

By 'token' he means 'proof': half a pound of sausages constituting proof not only of his desire to supply her with food but of his love for her.

We might also be struck by the extent to which Marten is involved in what he is doing for Mary. For a man who less than ten years before had been one of the ruling Council of England, he is wonderfully close to the everyday life of bread and sausage. But this corresponds to another thing that Aubrey discovered about him, how, in comparison with his political contemporaries, Marten was 'humble, not at all arrogant as most of them were'.[2] That helped him in his new life as a sometimes penniless prisoner.

The food he can organise is occasionally an indication of the time of year: 'half a chaldron of coles' and 'a quarter of a hundred of faggots' (*L* 53) are probably winter, just as the strawberries he sends her ('my chaps have watered for more') are summer (*L* 35) and 'some Plummes' (*L* 47), 'a parcel of fruit' (*L* 45) and those 'Bergamot pears from Holingbury' (*L* 58) are late summer or early autumn. Oranges (*L* 39, 51) are likely to be autumn, too. Vegetables are rare, only 'pease' (*L* 52), 'Hartichokes' (*L* 51) and 'Sparraguss' (*L* 29, 40), suggesting how seasonal they are, and how small a part they play in most people's diets. There are, regularly, candles, with the difference between 'cotton' and the cheaper 'rush' (or 'watch', used for watching) noted – he doesn't want anyone substituting rush for cotton – and also on one occasion (astonishingly) 'nine pound of soap' (*L* 18, 22). Mary must have had some extensive washing planned, as he noted when wearing a new (albeit second-hand) waistcoat, 'thy maid may be glad she has not the washing of the old one: for *I* believe it would take up more sope then *I* sent the other day' (*L* 18).

By far the most common – and year-round – commodities are bread, butter, and meat: 'two two-pennie loaves, two new rolls' (*L* 78), 'a sixpenny loaf from the market' (*L* 53), 'as much bread as took up every penny I had' (*L* 76), butter over and over again, but – most commonly of all – meat, whether 'Rabbets' (*L* 54), 'a piece of roasting Beef' (*L* 35), 'a piece of Venison' (*L* 58), the mutton previously listed, or – perhaps the smallest meal of all – a 'quarter of Lamb' on a day when he has nothing else to send (*L* 49). There is just the occasional break from the bread-and-meat diet, as when he talks of 'Fresh Salmon' and 'Gurnets' (*L* 54) – another kind of fish, sometimes called gurnard – or 'a piece of Sturgeon' (*L* 58), a present from a friend. It remains mysterious what the luxury might be 'contained in the brown paper' (*L* 41), of which he is careful not to cheat her – perhaps 'a scrap of Sugar' (*L* 51) or another 'piece of Cake' (*L* 58). We can, however, tell that, although Marten and Mary have both been more than once either on the verge of, or obliged to inhabit, the debtors' prison, they continue when possible to eat well and live well. Artichokes are, for instance, a relatively new import and not cheap, the drink sent out is commonly wine not beer, and Marten is insistent that the flour he sends Mary is 'not of 18d. the bushel' (*L* 14): good flour costs something like 50d. a bushel.[3]

We must not underestimate, either, the extent to which such cares of the everyday are necessary to such lives at such a time. After being in the Tower perhaps only a few days, weeks at most, when it becomes known that Richard Ingoldsby and John Hutchinson are supposed to be pardoned, Marten passes on to Mary Ward some extraordinarily hopeful gossip, probably from another prisoner, that they are (most of them) only to be banished,

> which if it be true, it is probable we shall have some time given us to provide our selves, and that is all the kindnesse *I* did ever expect, and more. (*L* 67)

Quite wrong – but it keeps the spirits up. Later on, after the Old Bailey trial, both would have been terribly conscious that a sentence of death – and what a death – might be imposed very soon indeed. But thinking of what might happen is perhaps pointless, and, as Marten touchingly tells Mary,

> thou and I will not talk of those matters, nor think neither (Shall we Love? ah that thou couldst help it!) till my Heart come to
>   Hers,
>   *H. Marten.* (*L* 33)

And, of course, they *do* think about 'those matters'. Marten

asks Mary, probably late in August 1660, if she could get a friend
to attend the Sunday sermon preached before the king, 'that is,
if possible, to get the knowledge of what is intended at Court
towards us, or some of us, and which' (L 46). But, although he
starts off another letter saying that 'I confess what I hear is not
very good', he is also determined to look on the bright side: 'the
best is like to be welcome whensoever it comes' (L 6). Common-
places of soap and bread and butter – all of them evincing the
loving care Marten would like to show to Mary and can sporadi-
cally manage – have their roles to play in helping them forget the
sword that hangs over Marten's head (a dead metaphor of awful
appropriateness).

※

To return to the everyday (as they were obliged to, over and over
again), a few goods come in to the Tower, too. One particular
servant, called Stephen, comes from Mary, and

> brought me a fine Nosegay, and Strowings, and some Lettice
> that he was fain to borrow, and scarce worth taking up;
> however *I* like his coming, to save the charges of a Porter,
> which *I* finde considerable, though he be a very honest fellow.
> Therefore let *Stephen* come again on Thursday morning, and
> no farther then the Butchers, who can better come to me then
> he. (L 14)

'Strowings' are herbs, especially welcome in the confinement
of the prison, and a nosegay of sweet-smelling flowers is very
acceptable for the same reason: Marten insists that Mary's letter
is nevertheless still 'the sweetest flower in the parcel' (L 15). But,
although Stephen is 'pretty well acquainted with the souldiers'
(L 75), there are restrictions on how far a servant is able to come.

Without special leave or the assistance of a warder he cannot
'pass the pikes' (*L* 31) and is therefore not allowed into the strictly
guarded part where Marten is confined, although the butcher
can apparently come. But servants are nevertheless sometimes
allowed in, and we find Marten telling Mary, shortly before she
plans to leave London for Derbyshire: 'I presume *I* shall obtain
leave for a sight of thee once at least before thou goest; for I got
it for Robin yesterday' (*L* 57), 'Countrey *Robin*' (*L* 8) being a
servant employed by Richard Peters, Marten's Derbyshire agent.

Who is allowed in (and out) of the Tower depends on the
arrangements a prisoner can make. In fact, almost anything
seems possible if one knows the right people and can make it
up to them appropriately. It will probably come as a surprise to
modern readers that a prisoner in the Tower might have one of
his children to stay with him, but although Marten would joke
about it – 'Buss all my Brats for me, and as thou hast conven-
iency send me one or two of them in a basket' (*L* 45) – he actually
manages to get them in at least once. He is anxious about his
youngest, Henryetta, who is teething, which has led her to scoff-
ing a piece of raw meat, hence her nickname of Bacon-hog: 'I
am glad to hear that the litle one will save you fuel for dressing
her meat, so she can have it raw: but I believe that was onely a
fit of her teeth which made her glad of the cold she found in the
raw flesh' (*L* 27–8). He now sends her some grapes, as something
soft, and he thinks about the nappies she needs; but he is also
planning how to take care of her middle sister Sarah to take the
pressure off Mary:

> *My Heart,*
> I Long to know how my poor little brat does after her grapes,
> that if they did well with her I might present her with more:
> mean while I present her bumm with a couple of Napkins, and
> claim thy promise of sending her Sister Sarah to me. (*L* 59)

Although the *Oxford English Dictionary*'s earliest date for the use of napkins (modern 'nappies') for children is 1842, that is what Marten must mean. But while Bacon-hog is only an infant, and Mary is in danger of being overwhelmed by the 'drudgery' of her current situation, he will take care of Sarah even when she is ill:

> Poppets Ague is turned into the sleeping disease I think, she will eat no meat, nor pottage made of meat, nor egge ... (*L* 25)

And yet she is 'well enough, and merry with a few humours, that *I* can make an asse of as *I* list'. He can make her laugh. There is also medicine he has forgotten to give her (as fathers forget): 'she has not taken her powder'. But she *will* take her powder, he reassures Mary, 'ere thou hear from us again'. It looks as if he also took Peggie in on one occasion.

Close relations can also come in, and Marten is very fortunate in having relations who are not only well off but who live near London and have estates. So, for example, his twenty-seven-year-old daughter Mall either brings or has sent from the estate at Great Hallingbury in rural Essex, which she and her husband (Thomas Parker, 2nd Lord Morley and Mounteagle) have inherited, on one occasion 'a Hollingbury hen' and on another at least three: 'I have also sent my three chits each of them a bird that came from Holingbury' (*L* 45). There are also 'some Bergamot pears from Holingbury' (*L* 58), 'a piece of Longworth Cheese, and a parcel of nuts from the same place' (*L* 63), '*Longworth* Pidgeons' (*L* 25), 'some *Longworth* Pig' (*L* 47) and that '*Longworth* commodity' (*L* 18). And these all go to Mary and the children as well as fruit 'that came a great deal further off, as this bearer can tell thee better then I' (*L* 45), perhaps from Derbyshire.

All the same, visitors also sometimes eat and drink up the

food which other visitors have provided, hence Marten's ironic comment that 'Here dines with me to day of her own invitation, and upon Malls victuals, my sister E—' (*L* 45) – that is, his sister Elizabeth Edmonds. On another occasion he ruefully tells Mary that his son-in-law 'my Lord M. and my daughter, and Jinny' – that is, Lord Morley and Mounteagle, Marten's fourth daughter Mall, and his seventh daughter Jane – 'brought 3 or 4 dishes of victuals and dined with me, but he got away all my wine that I had provided for thee, because he liked it' (*L* 36). Alcohol in one form or another is something else Marten constantly sends to Mary: bottles of sack (*L* 35, 41, 51, 52), Rhine wine (*L* 30, 51, 54), Canary wine (*L* 24, 58, 76), Claret (*L* 9, 73), beer (*L* 26, 75), simply 'liquor' (*L* 58). It seems possible that the Tower, too, boasted what many prisons illicitly maintained, a so-called whistling shop, where 'drams are privately sold'. It had perhaps been predictable how, back in 1650, when he had paid a visit to his newly acquired estates in Leominster, the only reference to him in the borough records had been an account 'for wine and metheglin [mead], bestowed on Coll. Marten. – 10s'.[4]

What is frowned upon most and is most difficult to arrange (but is also most desired) is a visit from Mary herself. This can only be managed when Robinson is out or away, but also with the complicity (doubtless paid for) of the gentleman porter and Marten's keeper, 'Master T—' (*L* 28): 'my Keeper has promised me afresh, that so soon as ever *I* am ripe for thee, I shall have one bout with thee here' (*L* 74). 'Bout' is sexual, as 'ripe' is also, in such a context. The fact that at some point Mary manages to leave her golden ear-rings behind in the Tower strongly suggests that she has taken them off during just such an encounter. Marten cheerfully writes to her afterwards that 'If any little mad girle have lost a small parcel of golden ear-rings, I know a cunning man will cast a figure for 'um, and use her reasonably' (*L* 25), that is, he will do an astrological calculation as to where they might be and not charge her too much, although 'use' inevitably also means have sexual intercourse with. In fact, they are returned to her by a trusted messenger: 'I have withall [moreover] sent thee thy Ear-rings, for fear I should make them march a wrong way, as I have heretofore made many a good thing' (*L* 64). Some letters are filled with longing:

> *Love and Dear,*
> I Do not thank thee for the hundred fine things thou sentst
> me last night by the woman, nor care for any thing thou hast
> done, or canst do, but coming to me ... (*L* 28)

There is another sexual invitation in the salutation at the end of letter planning an immediate visit:

> Here is 20 s. for thy Coaches earnest, if that businesse takes,
> and 5 s. for the Hack that brings thee hither to
> My Soul,
>   Thy Body,
>   *H. Marten.* (*L* 41)

However – either just before that visit or another one – things go dangerously wrong. Marten has had Sarah in prison with him, doubtless sent in by Mary after Marten claims 'thy promise in sending her' (*L* 59). Security had been tightened on numerous occasions, only for it to be relaxed again later: Marten comments about one 'new restraint' that 'I have outlived a hundred of 'um already, and am heart-whole still' (*L* 40). But when Mary writes confirming her visit – a letter also asking after Sarah – the woman chosen to bring it in, finding herself 'denied coming into the Tower', explains that she has 'a letter too for the Collonel' (*L* 27). The letter, being immediately opened, reveals to the warder who reads it the plans for Mary's illicit visit and also alerts him to the fact that Marten has a child sharing his prison lodgings. All potentially catastrophic … but because Marten is on such good terms with the gentleman porter, the matter gets hushed up. Only now his 'Keeper' warns him that he has to get Sarah out of the Tower as quickly as possible, and Mary will not be able to visit: 'Since I wrote thus far, Master *T*— advises me to rid away the girle so soon as ever *I* can conveniently, for the strictnesse encreases, though no body knowes any reason for it' (*L* 28). And that is managed; one of the servants or porters constantly travelling back and forth probably takes the child out.

But Marten still badly wants to arrange for Mary to get in: 'My Keeper and I are contriving how I may see somebodie else; but *I* will not tell thee who that is, because thou hast a shrewd guesse of thy owne' (*L* 15). And then comes their chance, on an occasion when Robinson is 'gone into the Countrey', leaving the gentleman porter in charge:

> therefore I hope to get leave of him for thee and my brats to dine with me on Wednesday: if it cannot be I will send thee word betimes that morning. If thou hearest nothing to the contrary thou may'st venture to come. (*L* 43)

This time arrangements are meticulous, down to the detail of Mary's disguise: she must 'make a rogue' of herself – that is, look like a servant, 'habited very plaine' (*L* 28, 70):

> then to take what guard thou wilt to the waterside, then a boat at what stairs thou wilt, that may bring thorow-bridge (the tide is ordered for the nonce) …

The boat should bring her to 'the by-ward about one of the clock', that is, to the thirteenth-century Byward Tower, the

Illustration 7: Tower of London, portcullis of the Byward
Tower: photograph by Benjamin Stone, 1898

principal gatehouse giving access to the Tower's outer 'ward' or
courtyard. Mary should 'come in with the crowd',

> but without thy brother or thy friend, or any body that has
> been seen with thee: nobody will take notice of thee there, but
> one, that stands there on purpose to bring thee off, if need be.
> In case thou hast a couple of Squires to conduct thee so far,
> thou may'st direct them to retire to the Angel or the Rose, or
> some such good neighbouring-place ... (*L* 28–9)

So the men will make their way to the nearest alehouse.

Almost the only question remaining is how many children
she will bring with her. The problem is poor little teething
Bacon-hog:

the little brat were best to be left behind, unless thou darest not trust it with its teeth out of thy company, then I hope it may do well enough to bring her, so thou hast some body to help thee carry her. (L 33)

Marten wants to see Bacon-hog, but leaves it to Mary to decide whether to bring her. Mary will, however, have to shed some clothes (she 'needs not be disguised for me') to prove that it is really her:

The care *I* take is for my own poor girle, that I am sure needs not be disguised for me; it is so long since *I* saw her, that *I* shall make her tell me some tokens [give me some proofs] before I believe it is shee, when *I* do see her. (L 29)

But 'the way is made, and the time to be about one of the clock, the manner as private as it was last time' (L 33).

※

Another day, another promise:

Tomorrow *I* shall send again, and if I do not so on friday too, it will not be because I did it 3 dayes together before: yet don't thou toil thy self to death with tending my brats, and scribbling to their father too; and of the two I can best abate thee the last office. I thank thee for my stew-pan, though his cap could not be found. *I* rest, My Heart,
    Thy own still, and still, and still,
        H.M. (L 50)

The reference to the 'cap' – lid – of his stew pan tells us that she must currently be in his lodgings and so with access to his cooking pots. Marten writes to her on another occasion 'be very careful, my Dear … of my couple of biddies, and of my study-doore key' (L 12). But either his or her lodgings are raided, probably late in 1661, when the letters are taken.

Why won't he be sending her anything on Friday? Because he will have no money left (a messenger to her will cost him a shilling). With his money normally arriving on a Monday it's going to be a tough weekend (although not as bad as when he writes how, 'though it be but Wednesday morning, I am at the bottome of my tubb' – L 22). And although he loves to hear from her every day ('at least of thee') yet if it's a choice for her between scribbling to him and tending to the brats, then it's not (for him) a choice. Even if he is thoughtful with regard to a woman with three children and little money, he also insists – 'My Heart' – that he is 'Thy own still, and still, and still' (L 50). Quietly and insistently. And he expresses himself with the acuity of a man knowing how dear she is (as she has been for years) but nevertheless telling her how his 'Masters' are responsible for her learning of the 'Dearness' which she might have preferred to have done without:[5]

> MY Dearest, that is, not dearer then other Deares, (for so thou wert forty years ago) but dearer then thou wert this morning, when *I* thought I could have sent to thee, and found *I* could not, therefore thou art beholding to my Masters for all that Dearness that thou mightst have spared. (L 39)

The endings of his letters are both clever and tender – hardly a single one of the eighty-nine exactly repeats the ending of another one. Each is written and meant, not just set down using standard phrases: 'Keep up thy poor heart, sweet Soul, a little while, though thou hast no reason for it, but for that *I* am ever and ever / Thy own, and no bodies else, / nor any thing else, /

H. M.' (L 19); 'Who am / Heart, / Thy / H. Marten' (L 28). Aubrey was the first to see how interesting it was that letters printed to embarrass and shame Marten were actually 'not to his disgrace', because they contain evidence of 'reall, naturall witt' and are also 'bôn naturel'.[6] A complete letter offers – if not food – yet intense anticipation. If Mary comes to the Tower 'upon the water', she will be crossing the Thames from Southwark, but more likely she will come 'by Coach' with two male servants ('thy hee-camerades'); the 'vitch' she might miss is 'victuals', food; 'bantlings' are small children, 'brats'. It's not the first time she has been 'Monkey-face' either, for he is 'a Monkey-faces / Owne, / H. Marten' (L 38): the insults being a way of drawing a cloak of intimacy around his mistress and himself and enclosing them within it.

> *My sweet soul,*
> Yea but I will see my own Dear to morrow, and all my little bantlings: for the Gentleman Porter has picked out that time to grant me thy company when Sir J— is sure to dine abroad, for he must not know it. I do not know whether thou darest venture thy baby upon the water or no; but the tide serves finely betwixt 11 and 12. If thou comest by Coach (which I think is the safest way) thou must set out an hour sooner, or else I shall eat up all the vitch before thou comest; for all that, I would have thy hee-camerades try their fortunes too. I will spend no more ink upon thee now, but bottle up all thy business for thy ugly ears. Therefore good morrow Monkey-face.
>   Thy
>   *H. Marten.* (L 32–3)

And then, early one morning when she is due later in the day: 'Thou dost not know how I have longed all night for this morning' (L 33). That letter dates from some time in September

1660, but neither he nor she knows just how close they are getting to his first public trial at the Old Bailey, which will start for him on Wednesday, 10 October. He will probably not hear about it himself until the evening before.

4

Procedures

The report of the October 1660 trial runs to 287 pages of print:

> AN *EXACT* and most *IMPARTIAL* ACCOMPT OF the
> *Indictment, Arraignment, Trial,* and *Judgment* (according to
> *Law*) of Twenty nine REGICIDES, THE *MURTHERERS* Of
> His Late SACRED MAJESTY ...

Various types and sizes and numerous sub-clauses extend the title
almost to the bottom of the page. 'His Late SACRED MAJESTY'
is, naturally, Charles I, whose last word on the scaffold in 1649
had been, simply, 'Remember'. The trial of the regicides was as
rich an effort of remembrance as might be imagined.

The twenty-nine individuals on trial at the Old Bailey, eleven
and a half years after the trial of the king, were all those who
could (in England and Wales) at that point be assembled and tried
as regicides. Of the fifty-nine commissioners who had originally
signed the death warrant, and the other seventeen commissioners who for one reason or another had not signed, twenty-four
were already dead, two dying; fifty remained as potential targets.
Four had, for complicated reasons, been pardoned; four more
were dealt with by the House of Commons; fifteen had got away
before they could be arrested and eventually died in exile: two
went into exile but came back; three escaped but were eventually
located, tricked, and brought back; two others escaped while

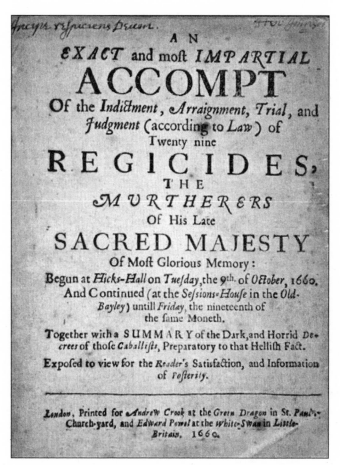

Illustration 8: Title page of *An Exact and
most Impartial Accompt* (1660)

in theory being held and also died in exile. In all, twenty-four
of the commissioners who had been listed as the king's judges
had either handed themselves in or had been tracked down and
locked up with the others in the Tower. And there they stayed
until October 1660 unless they happened to die in the meantime.
Five would die between 1660 and 1662, among them Vincent
Potter, who would be in a terrible state in court with 'a fit of the

Stone upon him', confessing 'I am not in a condition to declare what I know and would speak, I am mighty full of pain' (*EIA* 263). He was dead by February 1662.

Added to the twenty-four commissioners being tried in October 1660 were five other individuals who had assisted in condemning the king or worked at his actual execution. John Cooke was the lawyer who had conducted the case for the prosecution in January 1649 and who had written the king's indictment; Hugh Peters, although he had played no part in the trial, had preached Oliver Cromwell's funeral sermon and was accused of inciting regicide. The other three were soldiers seeing to the execution of the warrant: one – William Hewlet – accused of being the king's executioner (masked and wearing a wig on the scaffold), the second (Daniel Axtell) commanding the guards at the king's trial, the third (Francis Hacker) escorting the king to execution. Some other soldiers, although taking part in the procedures of the execution, had put themselves in the clear by signing nothing in 1649; some of them appeared as witnesses for the prosecution in 1660. Others who might have been tried, such as the clerks in court in 1649, had got away in time.

The *Accompt* – account – of the trial is an extraordinary document. It minutes not only most of what was said in court[1] but at times provides stage directions, like a play script, to show *how* the defendants spoke: '*I look for mercy from God*', said one, but the transcribers added 'and wept', as they did to another defendant who had just said '*I wish I could express my sorrow*'. He promptly did 'and wept' (*EIA* 275–6). The transcript is amazingly detailed, noting for example the judge's problems with hearing one defendant – 'I cannot hear you (he not speaking aloud)' (*EIA* 245) – and even transcribing the tricky pronunciation of a French witness:

Mortimer. Me Lar, me ha serd de King, &c.
Court. We cannot understand a word.
Coun. He is a Frenchman, my Lord.

And in spite of Dr Mortimer's further attempt to address the judge – 'Me Lar, me can peak Englis—' (*EIA* 164) – he is interrupted and told to sit down. The transcript also records the noises made by the public: 'Here the Spectatours *Hummed*', '*Here the people hum'd –*' (*EIA* 49a, 76). 'Humming' in this context was what a contemporary called 'a tumultuous hum',[2] sometimes an acclamation (the public roaring encouragement at counsel's attack on Thomas Harrison's behaviour to the king, for example), sometimes derision (as in their ridiculing John Carew's religious protestations). But such things were reproved by the judge: 'Gentlemen, This *Humming* is not at all becoming the Gravity of this *Court* … It is more fitting for a *Stage-Play*, then for a *Court of Justice*' (*EIA* 49a).

An implicit comparison with events on stage is, nevertheless, inevitable to those reading the *Accompt*. It records occasions where a defendant's attempts to speak or explain were interrupted; the printers' convention of using a dash to mark the occurrence of an interruption is employed. For example, a number of defendants refused to plead either guilty or not guilty, for various reasons, but were cut short in court. The man interrupting in the following case is the presiding chief justice of common pleas (one of the three overlapping court systems), Lord Chief Baron Sir Orlando Bridgeman. The slight change of direction in his sentence, as he says 'this is the course … the course is', is faithfully recorded:

Sir Hardress Waller. *My Lords, I dare not say,* Not Guilty; *but, since that in a Business of this nature, we have no councel or Advice, and being not able to speak to matter of Law –*

Lord Chief Baron. I am loth to interrupt you: but this is the course; you have heard the *Indictment* read, and the course is, you must Plead *guilty,* or *Not Guilty.* (*EIA* 21–2)

The *Accompt* also records details like the occasion when a witness simply glanced at one of the defendants (incidentally Henry Marten) in order to identify him, but the judge demanded a name to make sure the jury had grasped its significance:

Ewer, ... *I* followed that Gentleman, (looking at Mr. *Marten*)
I followed that Gentleman into that Chamber.
L. ch. B. After what Gentleman?
Ewer, Mr. *Marten,* my Lord ... (*EIA* 247)

Elsewhere, everyday exchanges are faithfully recorded. Thomas Harrison challenged juror after juror (he was allowed to do this, in a treason trial, up to the number of thirty-five); he was apparently trying to acquire jurors who were not upper class:

Mr Harrison. *May I not ask of what Quality he is?*
Court. No, Sir. (*EIA* 33)

Having got into the habit of challenging, however, he was tardy to realise that he should not have challenged Henry Edlin, Edlin's name revealing a man from a family of French Protestant refugees. A non-Church-of-England Protestant would not be a bad person for a Fifth Monarchist to have on his jury. The minutes record both Harrison's initial objection ('*I Challenge him*') and his immediate attempt to have Edlin '*Sworn*' as a jury member after all.

Henry Edlin called.
Mr. Harrison. *I Challenge him.*

Mr. Harrison. *Let him be Sworn.*
Court. No, No. *(Whereupon he was set aside.)*

Harrison attempted to explain, his stresses apparently marked
by non-italic type:

Mr. Harrison. *If I have any Apprehension, or knowledg, of
them, that's the thing, that leads me to it*: *as touching* this
man, he may be Sworn.
Court. When he is *Challenged*, he cannot be recalled. (*EIA* 34)

Having challenged others, Harrison was confronted by a potential juror about whom he could tell nothing, resulting in this
sardonic little exchange:

John Lisle was next called.
Mr. Harrison. *I do not know him.*
Mr. Lisle. Nor I you, Mr. *Harrison. He was Sworn.* (*EIA* 33)

At times the *Exact and most Impartial Accompt* reads exactly
like the 'Stage-Play' to which the judge had contemptuously
referred.

※

In that respect it is important to understand the layout of the
extraordinary stage on which most of this played out: the courtroom of the Old Bailey (then often called the Sessions House).
On 10 October 1660 the twenty-eight[3] accused had to plead
guilty or not guilty. Proceedings had actually started the previous
day, 9 October, at Hick's Hall in Clerkenwell. No defendants had
been present, but a grand jury had had the duty of pronouncing
whether there was a case to answer. This part of the process could

Illustration 9: Old Bailey, October 1660, taken
from *A Looking-Glass for Traytors*, 1660.

A: *The Lord major:* B: *The Comissioners:* C: *The Kings Councell:*
D: *The Sheriffs:* E: *The Clerks:* F: *The Jury:* G: *The Prisoner:* H:
The Witnesses: I: *The Bayl-dock:* K: *The Criers of ye Court:* L: *The
Keepers:* M: *The Stayre Case:* N: *The houses looking into ye Court:*
O: *Persons of Quallity Spectators within ye Court:* P: *The Common
people in ye outward yard:* Q: *The yard between the Court and ye Bar.*

be very serious: at a trial for high treason in 1681, for example,
members of the grand jury insisted that witnesses be examined
separately and not allowed to hear each other's testimony; following some serious cross-questioning, they declared the indictment
a Bill *Ignoramus*, meaning there was insufficient evidence for
a *Billa Vera* (a true indictment).[4] The trial ended forthwith. At
Hick's Hall in 1660, however, the grand jury announced a *Billa
Vera* without examining a single witness.

There appears to be no reliable contemporary image of the exterior or interior of the Old Bailey. What we do have is Illustration 9, a fascinating, although in many respects unreliable, picture appearing soon after the trial in a broadside sheet entitled *A Looking-Glass for Traytors*. This shows thirty members of the court at the back of the Old Bailey courtroom; they wear hats, which no one else in court does (other individuals wearing hats are outside the area of the court, at the bottom left and right of the illustration). In the courtroom itself are places to which *'Persons of Quallity'* have access, but *'The Common people'* ('P' bottom right in Illustration 9) – like the prisoners in the bail dock – have to remain outside, in Sessions House Yard, if they want to hear and see what is going on.

The illustrator also appears concerned to make his image of the Old Bailey in 1660 correspond to the layout of the trial of Charles I in 1649. As a result – like the king in Illustration 2 (see page xvii) – the guilty prisoner (marked 'G') is isolated at the very bottom of the picture, with his back to the brick-built back wall of the building, attended by those guarding him, his keepers (marked 'L'). In front of him stretches an open space up to the court itself. Furthermore, the two rows of judges at the top – as 'B' – are named *'The Comissioners'*, the name used for the judges at the king's trial in 1649 and only used at the trial in 1660 in references back to 1649. The bail dock, the outdoor area in which the prisoners were actually held before being brought up to the bar of the courtroom, should be behind where the prisoner 'G' is on trial, but in Illustration 9 it has been reduced to a meaningless little square area with spiked railings around it but no entrance and no one in it, marked 'I', at the bottom left. The bail dock for the Old Bailey was in reality exactly equivalent to the large open area in Illustration 9, with the prisoners awaiting trial being kept within it (Illustration 9 instead labels the individuals crowding around the bar 'H', *'The Witnesses'*).

The jury, labelled 'F' (six on each side; they were divided at this date) have also been removed from the courtroom. They have, absurdly, been relocated in the bail dock along with the prisoners held there.

To read the Illustration as the Old Bailey we need to bring the prisoner 'G' forward to the place marked 'H', which is the gate leading to the bar in the court, and also to bring the twelve jurors into the court, into the mass of people depicted in Illustration 9, but divided into two rows of six, one on each side of the judges.

Another example of the inauthenticity of Illustration 9 is demonstrated by its attempt to make the picture match the list of twenty-nine names of the court printed alongside it in the original broadside. Some of the court members there listed – such as John Montagu (created Earl of Sandwich on 12 July), Edward Hyde, now the lord chancellor, and General Monck (created Duke of Albermarle on 7 July) – the man generally credited as being most responsible for the return of Charles II – never attended the Old Bailey at all: they were only at the preliminary hearing on 9 October at Hick's Hall. The bureaucrat and diarist Samuel Pepys was much impressed by what the lawyer Henry Moore told him about the Hick's Hall assembly: 'such a bench of noblemen as had not been ever seen in England'.[5] The *Exact and most Impartial Accompt* actually lists twenty-nine significant figures at Hick's Hall: nobility, judges, and a few other notables, like the Lord Mayor of London. An identical list appears in *A Looking-Glass for Traytors*, and Illustration 9 shows thirty judges to correspond (at the Old Bailey there were, in fact, only eight judges). The creator ('I. C.') of Illustration 9 seems to have been working neither from life nor from his own sketch but from one probably scribbled by someone else and from what he had been told about the court and the numbers of people present.

Below the judges in Illustration 9 is, correctly, a table crowded

with court officials, among them the Clerk for the Crown, the
attorney general, the solicitor general, and other briefed lawyers
working for the prosecution. One was Sir Edward Turner, Attorney to the Duke of York (Charles II's brother); at an early stage
of the trial Turner was allowed to speak at length on behalf of
his client, condemning those who had murdered the king – his
client's father.

The rest of the very limited space inside the courtroom would
have been crowded with men called in for jury service, including a large number of extra potential jury members as well as
waiting witnesses. At times the press of people in the middle of
the court was so great that Bridgeman had to appeal to them
to move so that those being tried – up against the bar at 'H'
in Illustration 9, stationed 'for arraignment, trial, or sentence'[6]
after being brought forward from the bail dock – could actually see those being brought forward as potential jury members:
'*Gentlemen,* that are not of the *Jury,* Pray, clear the Passage. The
Prisoner is here for *Life,* and *Death*; let him have Liberty to see
the *Jury*' (EIA 35).

The most extraordinary feature of the Sessions House courtroom, however, both as it was in 1660 and as rebuilt after the
Great Fire (the law is notorious for not wanting things changed),
was the fact that it had no back wall but opened directly on to
the outside world and the bail dock. Illustration 10, dating from
1723–4, although showing the court as part of the rebuilt Old
Bailey, illustrates this beautifully. In Illustration 9, by contrast,
it is almost impossible to tell what is inside and what is outside
the courtroom. The comparatively small size of the Old Bailey
courtroom (in comparison with the bail dock in front of it) can
also be gauged in Illustration 10, which shows the swing gate
leading from the bail dock (open in Illustration 9) closed. The
courtroom itself looks like the inner stage of an old London
playhouse, with two great doors beside it, its audience outside

Illustration 10: *Justice Hall in the Old Baily*: print, 1723–4

in all weathers, and judges, counsel, and clerk having to work in a difficult, half-outdoors acoustic. They must all have learned to project their voices like actors – or the spectators outside would never have been able to react to court proceedings in the way they did. The open courtroom (which must have been freezing cold in winter) permitted trials to be interrupted by those outside; a hearing in 1681 was regularly punctuated by 'the Tumult' of the spectators, while – at the end – 'the People fell a hollowing and shouting'.[7] The building lasted in this open form until 1737, when protests from court officials finally led to the courtroom being enclosed.

The brick wall at the bottom of Illustration 10 is the external wall of the bail dock (also reproduced as a solid brick wall in Illustration 9), and within the dock in Illustration 9 – given some protection by capes but without hats – are five prisoners, one sitting despondently on the low wall at the back. The others are being introduced by a tall man also in a cape through the opening marked 'H' into the courtroom itself to line up against the 'Bar'. When they finally come before the court, they will be the only people not finely or carefully dressed; their status will be visibly degraded.

But perhaps the most impressive thing about Illustration 9 – and one of the valuable things about it – is the sheer number of people depicted; not just the rows of judges and nobility at Hick's Hall who so impressed Pepys but all kinds of extra persons. Around the lawyers' table are lawyers and clerks; there will also be replacement jurors (thirty-five extra ones needed for Harrison alone) and witnesses. And there are hosts of onlookers, packed into every corner and passageway and all around the outside of the bail dock. Illustration 9 is unrealistic in this respect, but it contains a graphic truth, and it is again aspiring to a parallel with the 1649 trial of the king and the huge number of onlookers then present.

While the proceedings at the Old Bailey lasted, prisoners (here not in chains, although that was the usual procedure) would be brought from their prisons to be kept 'out in front of the court in the bail dock all day (from 6:30 a.m. to 8 or 9 p.m.) during sessions, summer and winter, regardless of heat, rain, cold or snow'. From the bail dock, they 'could see and to a certain extent hear all that went on in the court'.[8] Towards the end of the 1660 trial one batch of prisoners – upper-middle-class men unused to standing about outdoors – protested, declaring *the place where they stood to be cold and unwholsome* (EIA 257). They were allowed back into Newgate Prison, just next to the Old Bailey, for the time being.

※

In 1660 the prisoners were brought from the Tower for the first day at the Old Bailey. Harrison started off in court by complaining bitterly about the lack of warning that he and the others had had of the trial, but while so doing he revealed the procedure used for getting them there on time:

> *Do you call me to give you a Legal Answer; not knowing of my Trial till nine of the clock last night, and brought away, from the* Tower, *to this place, at six of the clock in this morning.* (EIA 19)

He must have been roused between five and six – dark in mid-October, but proceedings at the Old Bailey began at seven in the morning at that time of year.

The court proceedings spelled out what happened next:

> SIR *John Robinson,* Knight, *Lieutenant* of his Majesties *Tower of London,* according to his *Warrant* received, delivered to Mr. *Sheriff* the Prisoners hereafter named; who were (in several Coaches) with a strong Guard of Horse, and Foot conveyed to *Newgate* ... (EIA 17)

It would have taken the coaches bringing Harrison and the others from the Tower around an hour to get there at walking pace, rumbling across the City of London in the gathering light, past Old St Pauls (still with shops tucked under Inigo Jones's classical portico – one of Marten's pamphlets had been 'sold at the *West-end* of *Pauls*') and so up to Newgate. Here they were 'delivered to the Keepers of that Prison'. Newgate Prison was next to the Old Bailey, and those now on trial were housed there. The Press Yard of old Newgate Prison was used as a holding pen for the prisoners before they were 'brought to the *Sessions-house* in the *Old-Baily*' (EIA 17): 'a way was made from the Press-yard backwards to the Sessions house, privately to convey them to and again, to keep them from the pressing of the people'.[9]

※

The judges were, technically, the 'Commission of *Oyer*, and *Terminer*' – they were thus (in old legal French) empowered to hear and give judgements in cases such as treason. When everyone was assembled, the official '*Indictment* was publickly read by *Edward Shelton* Esq; *Clerk of the Crown*' (*EIA* 17), one of the individuals at the lawyers' table with papers before him in Illustration 9. Among the clerk's duties in the small, crowded courtroom was responsibility for moving proceedings forward, in which he was assisted by two official Cryers – 'K' in Illustration 9 – who started off 'O yes, O yes, O yes' and bellowed out the court's orders at significant moments. While Harrison was being sentenced, for example, 'The *Cryer* made *Proclamation* for *Silence* whilest *Judgment* was in giving' (*EIA* 56), suggesting how noisy the courtroom got. Presumably to speed things up, defendants on the first day of the Old Bailey trial were brought forward in batches from the bail dock to record their pleas of guilty or not guilty:

> *Clerk*, Bring to the Bar *Isaac Pennington* Esq; *Henry Marten* Esq; *Gilbert Millington* Gentleman, *Robert Titchborn* Esq; *Owen Roe*, Esq; and *Robert Lilburn* Gentleman, Who were called, and appeared at the Bar, and, being commanded severally, held up their hands. (*EIA* 18)

These six, brought together but treated individually ('severally'), were distinguished either as 'Esquire' (meaning landed proprietor) or as 'Gentleman' (one whose means enable him to live in easy circumstances without engaging in trade). All, in fact, had – until recently – been successful upper-middle-class men, some of them extremely well known: three of them (Pennington, Marten, and Millington) MPs in the old Rump parliament, Millington a barrister, Rowe a prominent merchant who during the Civil War had been in charge of the armoury at the Tower of London, Lilburne a significant figure in the army during the Civil War and eventually governor of the city of York, Marten important in the army and as an MP and the son of the prominent judge Sir Henry Marten. Titchborne (knighted by Cromwell, chosen for Cromwell's short-lived House of Lords and one who believed that Cromwell should have declared himself king) and Pennington (on the 1649 Council of State with Marten) had in the past actually been Lieutenants of the Tower, where – until that morning – they had been held as prisoners; Pennington had not only once been Lord Mayor of London but had also preceded Sir John Robinson (who had just dispatched him as a prisoner from the Tower) as MP for the City of London. Sir Thomas Aleyn, the current Lord Mayor of London, having been one of the grand jury convened on the first day to push the case forward to its hearing, would now be heading the first 'petit jury' (twelve men) of the proceedings. In such ways, individuals like Titchborne and Pennington, men of the old regime, were being demonstrably stripped of rank and office as well as publicly humiliated.

※

All the accused were now facing the charge of high treason for being among the 'Pretended Judges' of Charles I in 1649. In the words of the court's indictment, each of them,

> *together with others, not having the fear of God before his Eyes, and being instigated by the Devil, did Maliciously,*

Treasonably, and Feloniously, contrary to his due Allegiance,
and bounden Duty, sit upon and condemn our late Soveraign
Lord, King Charls the First, *of ever Blessed Memory: and*
also did upon the thirtieth of January, 1648. *Sign and Seal*
a Warrant for the Execution of His late Sacred and Serene
Majesty, of Blessed Memory. (EIA 21)

They now faced not just the death penalty but – for high treason
– the most terrible possible public death. In the course of the
trial of twenty-nine defendants, Bridgeman spelled out the sentence ten times in all:

that *You be led back to the place, from whence you came,*
and from thence to be drawn upon an Hurdle[10] *to the Place*
of Execution, and there you shall be hanged by the Neck, and
being alive shall be cut down, and your Privy-Members to be
cut off, your Entrails to be taken out of your Body, and (you
living) the same to be burnt before your Eyes, and your Head
to be cut off, your Body to be divided into Four Quarters, and
your Head, and Quarters, to be disposed of at the pleasure of
the King's Majesty: *and the Lord have Mercy upon your Soul.*
(EIA 56)

Because such executions were always staged in public, there
was no way in which the executioner might (at the request of the
man's relations, appropriate bribes being offered and accepted)
have mitigated the terrible proceedings by, for example, cutting
the man down too late or ensuring that his neck was broken
when his feet were kicked off the ladder on which the executioner
would also be standing. (Guy Fawkes had famously interfered
with his similar execution in 1606 by jumping from the ladder
with the noose in place, thus breaking his neck.) Those who had
forced themselves to the front of the press of people wanted the

promised blood and (literally) guts, and the executioner would not have kept his job if he had not provided them. Pepys recorded how, after the first of the regicides were cut down in October 1660 then disembowelled and decapitated, the public response had been 'great shouts of joy'.[11]

Our modern sensibility would want to be reassured by the likelihood of there being a point at which the man would surely die (or at least lose consciousness) before the procedure was complete. But the past – as has been argued – 'is not a place for the squeamish',[12] and seventeenth-century sensibility wished for exactly the opposite: full consciousness down to the point at which the naked body, horribly mutilated but still alive, lying on a kind of raised execution board, was finally decapitated, its head being, as the climax of the whole, cut off and held up as the head of a traitor. Then came the quartering of the corpse, the bits and pieces either exposed on city gates or (just occasionally) returned to the relatives for burial: joyfully revengeful, religious royalist John Evelyn recorded how 'I saw not their execution, but met their quarters mangl'd & cutt & reaking [still warm] as they were brought from the Gallows in baskets on the hurdle: ô miraculous providence of God'.[13] The head (sometimes boiled in a cauldron to preserve it better) might also eventually be exposed on some public place: the *Exact and most Impartial Accompt* ends with some details of those who had been executed:

> The Head of *John Cook* is since set on a Pole on the North-East end of *Westminster-Hall* (on the left of Mr. *Harrisons*) looking towards *London*, and the Head of Mr. *Peters* on *London* Bridge. (*EIA* 286)

Cromwell's exhumed head would also later be exposed on the roof of Westminster Hall. The whole time the original court of justice trying Charles I in 1649 had been meeting, 'the *Heads* and *Quarters*' of some of the Gunpowder plotters had been 'yet hanging' on Westminster Hall.[14]

The public nature of the execution was another fact dictating how we should view it. Cutting off a man's sexual organs while he was still conscious necessitated his not wearing breeches of any kind, a shirt at most, but practicality meant nakedness: it was first the humiliation and then the utter degradation of prominent individuals that was being demonstrated, and all images of the procedures show the victim naked when finally on the execution board. The Scottish rebel William Wallace had been dragged naked on his hurdle to his execution in 1305, but those involved in the Gunpowder Plot, having failed to blow up king and parliament, are clothed in two January 1606 images of them being dragged to execution; they must have been stripped before being emasculated. The genitals of victims also had to be held up as a proof of what had been done, but the loss of blood caused by the severance would make the cutting open of the body and the dragging out of entrails a matter to be dealt with as fast as possible before the man lost consciousness.[15]

Sometimes the executioner would hold up the heart of the dead man (by then for sure dead) to declare it the heart of a traitor; there is at least one print of such a moment. This may have happened in October 1660, but the focus at Charing Cross, where the first eight executions took place, was for the hanging, emasculating, and disembowelling to take place in a large public space where the victim could be 'hanged with his face looking towards the Banqueting-house at *Whitehall*', where – as one frequently reprinted report insisted – 'our late Sovereign of eternal memory was sacrificed' (*EIA* 286), the final parallel with the events of 1649. A picture of one of the regicides on the execution ladder giving his final speech contains, in the background, a crude representation of the pilastered front of the Banqueting

Illustration 11: Regicide execution, Charing Cross: woodcut

House (not, in fact, visible from the Charing Cross of 1660, even down a long, straight Whitehall, but the man responsible for the woodcut had a point to make).

But Charing Cross was more central and inhabited than Tyburn, where such executions normally took place, and after four days of executions the locals protested: 'the stench of their burnt bowels so putrified the air, as the inhabitants thereabouts petitioned His Majesty there might be no more executed in that place'.[16] In an age when smells in the streets were normal, such a petition suggests just how appalling those fires and burnings of organs and excrement had become, and how much more worrying the stench was to the locals than the money that could be made from renting out window space upstairs. The final two executions took place at Tyburn.

The scaffolds, and all those on them or near them, would have at first been spattered then soaked and dripping with blood after just one execution. Macbeth in Shakespeare's play imagines with horror being 'seene with these Hangmans hands',[17] and people in the seventeenth century would have known exactly why.

Such executions were the backdrop to the Old Bailey's proceedings in October 1660. By the time the six defendants already mentioned, Messrs Pennington, Marten, Millington, Titchborne, Rowe, and Lilburne – all of them having pleaded not guilty the previous Wednesday – were brought out for their actual trial on Tuesday, 16 October along with nine others, ten of their fellow regicides had already been found guilty, and Harrison (on the Saturday) and John Carew (on the Monday) had been dragged on hurdles to Charing Cross and subjected to the procedures of execution. And while Tuesday's trial was actually going on, two other regicides (Hugh Peters and John Cooke) were being taken to Charing Cross. Four more would follow on the Wednesday, two more (at Tyburn) on the Friday. As Pepys commented: 'a bloody week this and the last have been, there being ten hanged, drawn, and Quarterd'.[18] He had attended the executions of Harrison and Carew. It was also reported that the king – who especially hated John Cooke for his confrontations with Charles I in 1649 – had witnessed a number of the executions (those of Scot, Cooke, Scrope, and Jones, Evelyn claimed[19]).

For every one of the men locked up for months at a time, eventually almost without warning brought to Newgate and the Old Bailey, and then – a year later – to the House of Commons, and finally to the House of Lords, more than twenty months after their first imprisonment in the Tower (and this in an age when justice was usually speedy, not to say immediate), their own extinction must always have seemed the most likely outcome. Marten was an impatient man who moved things on whenever he could, regularly abbreviating his words when writing ('bn p'sent' for 'been present', 'Ex:^{cy}' for 'Excellency', 'Clke' for 'Clerk', etc.), and being annoyed to discover that his Derbyshire mediator 'hangs an arse still [hesitates]' (L 21). He once commented that 'I was born to be killed by tediousnesse' (*L* 43). It may have been a tedious procedure to which they were all being subjected, but he must have reckoned he would be killed at the end of it, if not actually by it.

5

Old Bailey

There had been in all twenty-eight men held in the Tower on the charge of high treason, and when they were finally brought to trial at the Old Bailey (together with one more, last-minute addition), the prosecution – as it must have known it would be – was entirely successful. From twenty-nine trials it achieved twenty-nine death sentences, the result of proceedings that had been set up from the start to be a show trial of the kind hoped for by the author of *A Hue and Cry*.

The legal procedure in court consisted in dismissing out of hand all the arguments that individuals might have collaborated in the sentencing of the king to death because – as soldiers, for example – they had been under orders. One accused soldier urged, 'what I have done my Lord it hath been done only as a Souldier, deriving my power from the General' (*EIA* 198). But the presiding justice, Orlando Bridgeman, insisted that the argument 'that you did it *by command*' must be rejected: 'you must understand, that no power on earth could Authorize such a thing. No command in such a case can excuse you' (*EIA* 225). Various defendants tried to phrase (better than their predecessors had) how they had only been following the decisions of parliament – for example, that '*what was done, was done in the name of the* Parliament *of* England … *was done by their Power, and Authority*' (*EIA* 50) or because the trial of the king had followed a 'Commission from the Parliament' (*EIA* 67), or because

'*Whatever I did, be it more or less, I did it by the Command and Authority of a Parliamentary Power*' (*EIA* 89). The most finely judged of all these formulations – perhaps because it occurred comparatively late and the speaker had had the chance to hear what had been unsuccessfully argued by others – ran modestly as follows:

> my Lord, there was the House of Commons as I understood it: perhaps your Lordships think it was not a House of Commons, but it was then the Supreme Authority of *England*; It was so reputed both at home and abroad: My Lord, I suppose he that gives obedience to the authority in being *de facto*, whether *de jure* or no, I think he is of a peaceable disposition, and far from a Traytor. (*EIA* 249)[1]

This was Henry Marten, and it is cleverer than perhaps it looks: the Henry VII Act of Treason (the Book of *Primo Henrici Septimi*), cited more than once by Bridgeman (*EIA* 12, 176), protected those who adhered to a king *de facto*: here Marten claimed that there had been an authority of exactly that kind in 1649.

But his claim met only with a hasty dismissal in the solicitor general's address to the jury. For all the arguments offered by individuals on trial were trumped by two simple arguments from the prosecution. The first was that the parliament in 1649 had *not* been parliament (it being only a House of Commons without an effective House of Lords, and the Commons itself had been left in a savagely purged state). The second argument was that killing a king was illegal in any context, no matter who might have given the orders. There *was* no authority which could authorise such an action against a king. Bridgeman had made this clear during his very first speech to the grand jury on the first day of the trial when the accused were not present:

Gentlemen, Let me tell you what our *Law-books* say: for there's the Ground, out of which (and the *Statutes* together) we must draw all our Conclusions for matter of Government.

How do they Stile the *King?* They call Him, *The Lieutenant of God,* and many other expressions, in the Book of *Primo Henrici Septimi.* Saies that book there; *The King is immediate from God, and hath no Superiour.* The *Statutes sayes;* That *the Crown of* England *is immediately subject to God, and to no other Power.* (*EIA* 10)

Bridgeman also insisted that

The King can do no wrong, it is a *Rule* of Law, it is in our *Law-books* very frequent: 22d. of *Edward the Fourth*, Lord *Coke,* and many others. If he can do no Wrong He cannot be punished for any wrong. (*EIA* 13)

So not only was it God alone who could do anything against a king but the whole apparatus for putting the king on trial had actually been against the law.

It was natural that the prosecution should stress the God-given status of the king; divine right, as defined a century ago, 'was the form in which the seventeenth century stated the paramount duty of obedience to the law'.[2] But after 1660 English monarchs would never again quite believe they enjoyed the simple status of being 'immediate from God', no matter what language the machinery of government might use or how resonant such an idea of power would prove. It had, after all, been the army and parliament that had invited Charles II to come back to England to be its king. What mattered was that the idea of the monarch's absolute power, which had assisted in bringing down Charles I, should not reappear. And it did not.

The prosecution also depended on the nature of the charge of high treason. This did not involve harming the king personally (only the executioner had actually done that) but 'compassing and imagining his death' – that is, contriving it and imagining it. If it could be shown that in any way one had contributed to his death, this proved one's guilt; it followed that every one of the twenty-nine was inevitably found guilty. No other verdict was possible.

The procedures in October 1660 were, in the usual way of felony trials, heavily biased against the defendants. Not only was it made impossible for any rational defence to be mounted but, as usual in trials for treason, defendants were refused access to a lawyer (although there was very little that a lawyer could have done for them, given the attitude the court adopted towards possible defence strategies). Prosecution witnesses could also be neither challenged nor questioned, and at the Old Bailey in October 1660, the jury were barely allowed time to consult. It must have been decided beforehand which individuals should suffer capital punishment, even though their defence of themselves had in some cases been thorough and convincing and the evidence in other cases very slight.

The original sequence of events that had led to some individuals being exempted from the Act of Indemnity and others included had also been confused and at times palpably unfair; in some cases it had been driven by malice and self-interest. Colonel Adrian Scrope, for example, who, on payment of a year's income from his estates had been told he should have the benefit of the Act of Indemnity, had paid up in June 1660; the House of Commons had subsequently allowed him out on bail from the custody of the Serjeant at Arms. In August, however, he had found himself excluded from the Act of Indemnity because of something conveniently recollected by Lord-Mayor-of-London-elect Sir Richard Browne and told to members of the House of Commons in August. The Parliamentarian and regicide Edmund

Ludlow was shocked by 'That apostate Browne', 'this trappan-
ner'[3] (one who ensnares and entraps), who thus single-handedly
had got Scrope excepted.

Browne had once been a distinguished major general in the
Parliamentarian Army[4] and had remained an MP in all Cromwell's parliaments – something which men like Marten had on
principle refused to be. But Browne had then turned against the
Commonwealth and had begun 'to designe the way of his pre-
ferment' by agitating for the return of the king. He had been
knighted in March 1660 and in April had been elected MP for
the City of London for the so-called Convention parliament; he
met and greeted Charles II when the latter arrived in London and
led the triumphal procession.[5] For this Browne had quickly been
created a baronet, on 22 July 1660. Such a progress was much too
much for a believer in the Cause like 'Levelling *Ludlow*'.[6]

What Browne alleged was enough for Scrope to be exempted
from the Act of Indemnity and sent for trial. In court, although
he confessed that he no longer recalled his own words, Browne
provided this evidence for the prosecution:

> upon some occasion I was accidentally at the Chamber of the
> Speaker, there I met this Gentleman whom indeed I knew not;
> he told me who he was; and when I understood who he was, I
> said to him (or words to this purpose, I cannot tell the words)
> because I would not distaste him, and say *you* have done this,
> therefore I put it thus: *We* have done this, What a sad case have
> *we* said I brought this Kingdom unto? Why, saith he? you see,
> said I, how it is ruined now the King is murthered, *&c,* Saith
> he *some are of one opinion, and some of another.* Sir, said
> I, do you think it was well done to murther the King; saith
> he, *I will not make you my confessor, Sir,* it was much to this
> purpose. (*EIA* 65)

No other evidence was offered, but there was no need for any, given Browne's eminent position in society, and also because those charged were not allowed to cross-question those who gave evidence against them. The list of exemptions from the Bill of Indemnity, which had originally been limited in the House of Commons (in mid-May) to just seven individuals but by 12 June had been enlarged to twenty, grew to include – or to be entirely accurate, to except from the Act of Indemnity, as finally agreed by the Commons on 11 July – twenty-eight.

The summer of 1660 had seen major changes in the British establishment from one body of important people to another. Orlando Bridgeman, an exact lawyer and experienced conveyancer who had served under Cromwell but had kept a very low profile, had on the very day that Charles II had arrived in London been appointed Chief Justice of Common Pleas to replace Lord Chief Justice Oliver St. John, who had served under Cromwell (and this although St. John had refused to serve at the king's trial in 1649 and had worked with Monck to bring Charles back). Extraordinary contradictions and confrontations inevitably developed: John Cooke, one of the great lawyers of his time (indeed, of any time), who had been solicitor general up to May 1660, found himself in October 1660 indicted for high treason by his successor as solicitor general, Sir Heneage Finch.

Edmund Ludlow's long narrative of events – not to be trusted in many details, written as it was by a man who had escaped the new regime and remained utterly antagonistic to it – renders the events of the first six months of 1660 both terrifying and deeply absurd, as it shows the factions' disputes and the unfairness and illegality of much that occurred. It so happened that the matter of the king's judges was raised in the Commons on 12 May, some two weeks before Charles actually returned, and a number of sitting MPs named as commissioners in 1649 took their chance: Richard Ingoldsby, for example, 'confessed his fault with great penitence, and desired the mercy of the House, which he will undoubtedly have', wrote another MP. Ingoldsby's friend the Earl of Northampton had already written to Charles II about him, saying that Ingoldsby wanted only 'His majesty's pardon and forgiveness of former errors'.[7] And Ingoldsby – who had been promoted by Monck – was never charged with anything: he would actually be made a Knight of the Bath at Charles II's coronation. Others in the same situation were not able to clear their names in the same way; and almost every day during June and July the numbers and names of those 'to be exempted from pardon' changed. On 7 June, for example, five names were added to the 'seven in the book'.[8]

Scrope had handed himself in to the House of Commons before the deadline in June 1660, and no other individual who did that suffered execution.[9] It would be Browne's testimony alone of what he alleged Scrope had said – something of which Scrope had no recollection – which meant not only that Scrope was excluded from the Act of Indemnity but was executed. The fact that he was included in the first ten to be put on trial is a sign that the prosecution had previously decided that Browne's testimony would count against him and that it would be fatal for him.

The case of the commissioner Thomas Wogan was an example of unfairness the other way around. Wogan had only attended on three days towards the end of the king's trial, but he had signed and sealed the death warrant. He had handed himself in late (on 27 June 1660) to the Serjeant at Arms but never seems to have got to the Tower of London, where by August all the other prisoners of the Serjeant at Arms had arrived (the Lieutenant of the Tower would declare on 7 February 1662 that Wogan 'never was in his Custody'). Most remarkably of all, Wogan was not put on trial in October 1660 either; his next appearance in the surviving record is when some member of the House of Lords in

February 1662, looking for extra candidates for execution (and perhaps checking the list of signatories to the death warrant), attempted to have him summoned to attend the Lords. But Wogan was in prison in York and never appears to have been brought to London, and he escaped from York to the Continent in 1664. The last heard of him is (perhaps) in Pembrokeshire in 1669. It seems most likely that he had influential friends, probably in the Commons, who helped get him off the hook and out of London during July or August 1660, although how the deal was done consigning him to gaol is a mystery.

Of the first eleven to be tried in October – six of the fifty-nine 'Commissioners' who had signed and sealed the death warrant, three soldiers who had attended his execution and two other individuals (the king's prosecutor John Cooke and Hugh Peters) – ten had had the sentence of hanging, drawing, and quartering carried out by the end of the second week of the trial. None of those on trial was allowed access to a lawyer, although quite a number of them had legal experience (Cooke had actually prosecuted the king in 1649). But nothing that was argued in court or offered as defence would prove of any use at all, as each individual, in turn, found out. Marten's belief that, as defendants, they would have to 'fence for their lives with Masters in the Art, and their Masters too' (L 2) was quite unfounded: their 'Masters' had no intention of fencing with them. Cooke's arguments in his own defence were brilliant – and totally ignored.

The offenders who would be executed immediately, no matter what was said in court, had been singled out either because of the roles they had played (like Cooke and Peters) or because they had not handed themselves in during June to be candidates for mercy or because – as with Scrope – a particular reason to make an example of them had emerged.

※

In some ways the most memorable of the twenty-nine trials was the very first – and longest. The prosecution had singled out Major General Thomas Harrison as first up. He was a man of forty-four, so younger than others, with a distinguished military career; on 11 November 1647, though, he had described Charles I as 'a Man of Blood' who ought to be prosecuted and not negotiated with. Those remarks were one of the reasons for the king's flight from Hampton Court to the Isle of Wight in search of security. The phrase was taken up by others: Adjutant General William Allen, for example, recalled army officers on 29 April 1648 resolving that 'it was our duty, if ever the Lord brought us back again in peace, to call *Charles Stuart*, that man of bloud, to an account'.[10] Men such as Harrison would have been very aware of the scriptural grounds for using such language:

ye shall not pollute the lande wherein ye are: for blood, it defileth the land: and the land cannot bee cleansed of the blood that is shed therein, but by the blood of him that shed it.[11]

Harrison had been put in command of the military escort that brought King Charles back to London in January 1649. The king, with good reason, had feared what Harrison might do but had found him courteous and entirely correct: Harrison was not a murderer but a professional soldier in charge of a prisoner.

He was, however, a millennial Fifth Monarchy man: Illustration 12 reproduces the title page of a twenty-page pamphlet explaining, in short form, what Fifth Monarchists expected to happen on the death of Charles I (which they interpreted as the end of the Fourth Monarchy). The 'Saints of the Most High', 'the people', were coming to power, and Christ would return to commence the Fifth Monarchy: there could be no other earthly monarch (Charles II would thus be a usurper). Over the years Harrison would quarrel with almost everyone but was a soldier

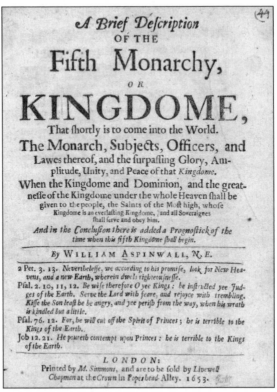

Illustration 12: Title page of William Aspinwall, *A Brief Description of the Fifth Monarchy* (1653)

of great experience and courage and a man of total integrity, respected if not sympathised with. To dismiss him as simply a Puritan fanatic is absurd.[12] Like Marten, he had been selected for the Council of State in 1649; in 1653, after an abortive attempt to establish the 'rule of the Saints' in the 'Barebones' parliament, Harrison fiercely opposed Cromwell's adoption of the Protectorate; he would end up imprisoned on numerous occasions between 1653 and 1658.

In May 1660 Harrison made no attempt to hide from what he knew was coming (in earthly terms) but let himself be arrested.

One MP wrote to a friend that 'Coll. Harrison scorns to ask pardon; he saith the Protector kept him in prison a great while, and now the King is come he will take away his life and ease him of that trouble'. Harrison had actually been imprisoned in the Tower in May – permitted 'to have One Servant with him, under the same close Restraint with himself'[13] – and had therefore been there longer than anyone else. On 5 June he had been selected by the House of Commons to be the very first of the (then planned) seven persons to be excepted out of the Act of Pardon, Indemnity and Oblivion. The prosecution in October was probably hoping that by putting on trial a man obviously guilty and regarded as a savage extremist his condemnation would make subsequent trials more straightforward.

Harrison's hearing took the longest of all, but he made every possible objection. His awkwardness started before the trial had even begun. The clerk saw to it that the first three prisoners were brought in to plead guilty or not guilty:

Sir *Hardress Waller,* Collonel *Thomas Harrison,* and Mr. *William Heveningham* were brought to the *Bar,* and commanded to hold up their Hands: which Sir *Hardress Waller,* and Mr. *Heveningham* did; but *Harrison,* being commanded to hold up his Hand, answered, *I am here*: and said,
My Lord, if you please, I will speak a Word –
Court. Hold up your hand, and you shall be heard in due time.
Mr. *Harrison,* the course is, That you must hold up your hand first. *And then he held up his hand.*
The Indictment was read ... (*EIA* 20)

Harrison had trained as a lawyer; he knew what was expected by the court. He was laying down his marker. This moment's difficulty was only a preparation for what would follow. Waller – after some to-ing and fro-ing – agreed to plead not guilty, but

Harrison constantly refused to plead, in spite of the threats that if he refused to do so he would be set down as pleading guilty. He insisted that, being deprived of legal representation, he was unable to plead; he insisted on being allowed to speak to the court; he demanded that the court give him advice about his case. This went on and on. Finch as solicitor general tried to deal with the matter, asking the judges:

> **Mr. Sol. Gen.** I *do beseech your Lordships, he may Plead. Per-adventure he knows his case so well; that he thinks it as cheap to defie the Court, as Submit to it.* (EIA 20)

This meant that he knew he hadn't a chance of winning his case so had decided simply to be awkward. But Harrison went on regardless, until, finally, stating: '*You do deny me Councel, then I do plead* Not guilty' (EIA 20).

But even then he wasn't done. He was obliged to say that he wished to be tried by God and his country. He wouldn't say it. 'I will be tryed according to the Laws of the Lord'. That kind of language was not acceptable to the court, not at all. Again a long argument, with this kind of exchange:

> **Clerk.** How will you be Tried.
> **Th. Harrison.** *I will be tried according to the ordinary course.*
> **Clerk.** Whether by God, and the Countrey? You must speak the Words.
> **Th. Harrison.** *They are vain words ...* (EIA 24)

... when we feel that he is both terribly right, according to his own beliefs, but that he is also finding an excellent way to play for time. In the end he says it in his way, and the clerk, in relief, rounds off the exchange with the official formula:

Clerk. How will you be tried?

Th. Harrison. I *do offer my self to be Tried in your own way, by* God *and my* Countrey.

Clerk. God send you a good deliverance. (*EIA* 25)

And all that was simply the business of getting him to make his plea; his trial had not even started.

Harrison was a shrewd man who would quickly have become aware that he had no chance of convincing the court or the jury that he should not be found guilty. But he was not only playing for time. He was going to use the resources of justice against the unjust nature of the court, where decisions about guilt had been decided beforehand. He enjoyed making things as difficult as possible; he would fight to stay alive, as he had always fought.[14] A contemporary account of the trial reported that

> Major General *Harrison* in his Pleadings carried himself so confidently to the Court as if he thought himself Carelesse and Unconcerned in the businesse: and seemed to justifie not onely the Power under which he Acted but also the Act it self, saying that Kings had formerly been privately Assassinated and Murthered, but what they had done was in the Face of the Sun and in the Fear of the Lord ...[15]

Someone who was in court reported that

> noe other could be heard this day: with much assurance and glory he avowed the fact, and spake as much treason and blasphemy now as he had acted before; he said he had often pray'd with tears that God would direct him, and it was revealed to him to be a just action to put the King to death, who (he said) had made war against the Parliament, and was guilty of all the bloodshed in the war ...[16]

Nothing he could offer in the way of such argument, however, was any use at all, although it took a whole day of jury challenges, repetitions, and wranglings before the court could conclude, with a short retirement of the jury, a sentence of death, 'and he was immediately sentenc'd to be hang'd, drawn and quartered; after this he went away smiling without any appearance of trouble'.[17] No one else showed his confidence and assurance, but exactly the same conclusion was reached for each of the first ten defendants.

※

Marten came up for trial the following Tuesday; his trial was a great deal shorter than Harrison's but significant in its own way.

> **Clerk**. *Henry Marten.*
> **Counsell**. He did both sign and seal the precept for summoning the Court, and the warrant for Execution, sat almost every day, and particularly the day of sentence.
> **Marten**. My Lord I do not decline a confession so as to the matter of fact, the malice set aside, *maliciously, murderously, & trayterously.*
> **Counsell**. If you have any thing to say to that, we will prove it. (*EIA* 245)

At this point, Bridgeman weighed in and attempted to show how ignorant of the law Marten was; he cannot have reckoned with the quick-wittedness of the prisoner in front of him (in comparison with whom Bridgeman's words go around in circles and are never very clearly expressed).

> **L. Ch. *Baron*.** That I may inform you in it, there is malice implied by law, malice in the act it self, that which you call

malice, that you had no particular intention or design against the Kings person, but in relation to the Government, that will not be to this present business; if it should extenuate any thing, that would be between God and your own soul, as to that which is alledged in the indictment, *Maliciously, Murderously, and Trayterously,* they are the consequences of law. (*EIA* 245)

Finch, the solicitor general, joined in here, too, with a witticism about Marten's confession, doubtless hoping for laughter from the lawyers (obliged to laugh when the solicitor general cracked a joke) and from the public:

> **Mr.** *Solicitor General.* My Lord, he does think a man may sit upon the death of the King, sentence him to death, sign a warrant for his Execution, *meekly, innocently charitably, and honestly.* (*EIA* 246)

Marten took the best possible line with Bridgeman and Finch: straightforward deference (however tongue in cheek) followed by the unsheathing of a rather sharper legal brain than was being applied to him. He may, in fact, have been the 'Henry Marten' admitted to Gray's Inn in August 1618, and earlier in 1660, perhaps in August, he had – in the letter 'arraigning my selfe at the bar of my own conscience' (*L* 1) published in 1662 by Gayton – rehearsed these very arguments about murder and malice and the law.

> *Marten.* I shall not presume to compare my knowledge in the Law with that of that learned Gentleman, but according to that poor understanding of the Law of *England,* that I was capable of, there is no fact that he can name that is a crime in it self, but as it is circumstantiated. Of killing a watchman,

as your Lordship instanced, a watchman may be killed in not doing his office, and yet no murder. (*EIA* 247)

That is, it's not murder if a watchman is killed for not doing what he should. This provoked quick, wordy back-pedalling from Bridgeman:

> **Lord Chief Baron.** I instanced that of a watchman, to shew there may be a malice by Law, though not expressed, though a man kill a watchman, intending to kill another man, in that case it is malice in Law against him: so in this case, if you went to kill the King when he was not doing his office, because he was in prison, and you hindred him from it, the Law implies malice in this. (*EIA* 247)

And then, as an afterthought, he had to agree with Marten, but then he came back with the killer blow against which no argument would work:

> it is true, all actions are circumstantiated, but the killing of the King is Treason of all Treasons. (*EIA* 247)

And to make up for Bridgeman's wandering away from the point, one of the other judges, Lord Justice Foster – who had previously only briefly joined in the proceedings – decided to settle the matter and show Marten how wrong he was:

> **Justice Foster.** If a watchman be killed it is murder, it is in contempt of Magistracy, of the powers above; the Law sayes, that contempt adds to the malice. (*EIA* 235)

And yet another lawyer for the Crown joined in as well:

Councel. We shall prove against the prisoner at the Bar (because he would wipe off malice) he did this very merrily, and was in great sport at the time of the signing the Warrant for the King's execution. (*EIA* 235)

Again doubtless hoping for (shocked) laughter. To which Marten could only reply, very justly, 'That does not imply malice.' (*EIA* 235)

But the Crown had an extremely hostile witness standing ready, a man supposed once to have been a servant of Marten's. It has proved impossible to identify him further than to give his first name as 'Robert'.[18]

Ewer sworn.

Councel. Come Sir, you are here upon your Oath, speak to my Lords and the Jury, you know the prisoner at the Bar very well, you have sometimes served him, were you present in the painted Chamber 29. *January.* 1648. at the signing the Warrant the Parchment against the King?

Ewer. The day *I* do not remember, but *I* was in that chamber to attend a Gentleman there, *I* followed that Gentleman, (looking at Mr. *Marten*) *I* followed that Gentleman into that chamber.

After Bridgeman had ensured that everyone knew who 'that Gentleman' was, Robert Ewer came out with his accusation:

Ewer, ... My Lord *I* did see a Pen in Mr. *Cromwell*s hand, and he marked Mr. *Marten* in the face with it, and Mr. *Marten* did the like to him: but I did not see any one set his Hand, though *I* did see a parchment there with a great many seales to it. (*EIA* 236)

But that, apparently, was that – no further lawyerly comment seemed necessary, although the anecdote would become the most talked about incident of Marten's life, eliciting comments on the way in which Marten and Cromwell inked 'one another's faces like schoolboys' and how 'Cromwell and Marten had cheerily spattered each other's faces as they signed the death warrant'.[19] But marking a man in the face with ink is not at all the same as spattering ink; scratching a black cross on his cheek would, for example, be macabre and not just funny. But – if indeed it happened – the incident seems likely to have been neither cheery nor schoolboyish but to have resulted from wild astonishment at the extraordinary thing they were doing.

The prosecution had lined up another witness against Marten, Sir Purbeck Temple, and went straight on to his evidence. He claimed to have overheard discussions between Cromwell and others just before the trial of the king, when Cromwell – in something of a panic, according to Temple – had asked the assembled group:

> let us resolve here what answer We shall give the King when he comes before us, for the first Question that he will ask us will be; by what Authority and Commission we do try him? To which none answered presently. Then after a little space Henry Marten the Prisoner at the Barr rose up, and said, in the name of the Commons and Parliament assembled, and all the good People of England, which none contradicted, so all rose up … (EIA 248)

Again, there is no confirmation (and Temple's story of just happening to be next to a hole in the wall behind the hangings of the Painted Chamber, when he just happened to overhear it, is very dubious indeed), but when it was put to Marten he did not deny it, he may even have been pleased that someone remembered it.

It had, in fact, become a crucial formula for the prosecution. The claim that it was in the name of 'the people of England' or of 'the good people of England' that Charles had been put on trial was repeated over and over in 1660, by four different prosecution witnesses, by the King's Counsel, by Orlando Bridgeman on numerous occasions (*EIA* 111, 113, 129, 131, 138, 139, etc.). All these repetitions occurred long before Temple claimed in the court to have heard Marten invent the phrase and before Marten, in turn, confirmed his belief that the commission 'went in the name of the Commons assembled in parliament, and the Good People of *England*' (*EIA* 249). He was, however, the only one of the accused to use the phrase. It must previously have been impressed upon the memories of the prosecution witnesses, as well as on those of the judge and the prosecutors.

Temple then proceeded to ramble on into another long anecdote about Marten being responsible for stealing horses from the royal stables:

> **Sir P. Temple,** At another time I was in Town on a *Friday,* and wanting Horses, I went to *Smithfield* where I saw the Horses of State of his late Majesty to be sold in the Common Market … (*EIA* 248–9)

Counsel had to shut him up with a simple question:

> **Councel.** *Was this before the Trial?*
> **Sir P. Temple.** It was in 1642, or 1643.

It was therefore useless as evidence. Counsel wanted to break off the whole of this meandering testimony – '*That's nothing to this business*' (*EIA* 249) – but was not quick enough to stop Marten, who had had time for a moment's thought, getting in yet another shrewd punch:

Marten. My Lord, the Commission went in the name of the Commons assembled in Parliament and the good people of *England*, and what a matter is it for one of the Commissioners to say, let it be acted by the *good people of England*? (*EIA* 249)

Meaning, 'What's your problem with someone in my position saying, "Let the good people of England do it"?' All Finch could do was to get heavily moral:

Mr. Soll. Gen. You know all *good people* did abhor it, I am sorry to see so little repentance. (*EIA* 249)

But that only gave Marten the chance to get back in again with another approach altogether:

Mar. My Lord, I hope that which is urged by the learned Councel will not have that Impression upon the Court and Jury that it seems to have, that I am so obstinate in a thing so apparently ill; My Lord, if it were possible for that blood to be in the body again, and every drop that was shed in the late wars, I could wish with all my heart: but my Lord, I hope it is lawful to offer in my own defence, that which when I did it, I thought I might do ... (*EIA* 249)

And at that point Marten managed to point out that the House of Commons in 1649 still *was*

the Supream Authority of *England*; It was so reputed both at home, and abroad ... (*EIA* 249)

Marten crowned his speech with the ingenious argument that in 1649 the king was no longer actually king:

My Lord, I shall humbly offer to consideration, whether the King were the King indeed, such a one whose peace, Crowns and Dignities were concerned in publick matters: My Lord, he was not in execution of his offices, he was a prisoner. (*EIA* 250)

It was a little surprising that he had been allowed to go on so long, or so precisely, but he brought his speech to an end with a beautiful series of compliments – and the confession that he was a convinced Commonwealth man, but, of course, he would be obedient to Charles II, if the latter chose to pardon him:

My Lord, I will not defer you long, neither would I be offensive, I had then and I have now a peaceable inclination, a resolution to submit to the Government that God hath set over me. I think his Majesty that now is, is King upon the best title under Heaven, for he was called in by the Representative body of *England*. I shall during my life long or short, pay obedience to him: Besides, my Lord, I do owe my life to him, if I am acquitted for this. I do confess, I did adhere to the Parliaments Army heartily, my life is at his mercy; if his Grace be pleased to grant it, I have a double obligation to him.

This – especially the bit about his adhering heartily to the parliament's army – must have left the court a little anxious about how to respond, and Sir Heneage Finch cautiously chose to boot the speech (and all the points it had made) into the long grass – that is, back to the House of Commons – for them to handle. He was either being extremely ironical about 'the people' or he was apparently accepting what Marten was saying:

Mr. Soll. Gen. My Lord, this Gentleman the prisoner at the bar, hath entred into a discourse, that I am afraid he must have an answer in Parliament for it. He hath owned the King, but thinks his best title is the acknowledgment of the people and he that hath that, let him be who he will, hath the best title: we have done with our evidence.

In other words, stop there, don't listen to anything else. But Marten was again too quick and turned himself into a thorough-going monarchist rather more concerned to stand up for Charles II than the court had been. If he himself were to be acquitted, that would not mean that the Crown was 'Cast' – that is, defeated in a legal action. Once again, Marten had a good deal more legal language available than he had pretended:

> *Marten.* I have one word more, my Lord, I humbly desire that the Jury would take notice, that though I am accused in the name of the King, that if I be acquitted the King is not Cast: it doth not concern the King that the prisoner be Condemned, it concerns him that the prisoner be tryed, it is as much to his Interest, Crown, and Dignity, that the Innocent be acquitted, as that the nocent be condemned. (*EIA* 250)

He thus beautifully positioned himself as one of the 'Innocent' whom the king would wish to acquit. The 1698–9 John Toland version of Ludlow's *Memoirs* comments on Marten showing, in these statements to the court, 'as much presence of mind as solidity of argument',[20] and that puts it very well.

But in court Finch knows he must say something else; he has *not* after all brought a very clear case to a very clear conclusion. Having accused the prisoner of entering into a discourse, he enters into a far longer one himself:

> *Mr. Sol, Gen.* My Lord, this puts us now upon the reputation of our evidence, and you may see how necessary it is to

distinguish between Confidence and Ionocence, for this very
person that desires you to have a care how you condemn
the innocent, he doth seem to intimate to you, that he is
an innocent person at the bar; and yet confesses he did sit
upon the King, did sentence him to death, that he signed the
Warrant for the execution, and yet here stands that person
that desires you to have a care of condemning innocence:
what is this at the bottome of it, but that my fact is such as
I dare not call it innocence, but would have you to believe it
such. (*EIA* 250–1)

Finch has got himself fairly tangled up; that last sentence is
impossible to follow. He has to start again: the thing to do is
to begin 'Gentlemen of the Jury' and hope that everything will
follow properly.

Gentlemen of the Jury, was it your intention the King should
be so tryed, as this prisoner moved? (*EIA* 251)

That is seriously odd. The prisoner had never suggested how the
king should be tried. Finch is flailing. All he can do is tell the jury
what they ought to think:

it will concern you to declare that the People of *England* do
abhor his facts and principles, every fact the prisoner hath
confessed himself, the sitting in that Court, which was treason;
his sentencing was treason, signing the Warrant for Execution
was the highest of treasons: Gentlemen, all that he hath to
say for himself is, there was an authority of his own making,
whereby he becomes innocent; But we hope out of his own
mouth you will find him guilty. (*EIA* 251)

What the jury will make of the idea that Marten had an authority that he had invented to make himself innocent, goodness knows. Not many will follow that.

Bridgeman then has to sum up, and his way of doing so is to explain that Marten and the seven on trial together with him are all guilty; they must be, there is no way they cannot be. The jury are nevertheless a little troubled. The *Exact and most Impartial Accompt* records that, following Bridgeman's would-be plain-as-plain statement (actually an order) that 'the fact is confessed by them all. It is so clear you need not go from the Bar' – signifying that the jury have no need to consult; in fact, they ought not to – all the same they do go ahead and consult. It is simply not true that 'the fact is confessed' by all eight defendants, except in the very special sense that the court has given to 'fact' (it being a fact that the sacred monarch is dead, and it being a fact that the regicides compassed it). But confession means confessing guilty: all eight have actually pleaded not guilty, and Marten in particular has managed an excellent defence. The clerk actually breaks into the silence as the jurors take their places again.

> After a little Consultation between the Jurors, they returned to their places. –
> *Clerk of the Crown.* Are you agreed of your Verdict?
> **Jurors.** *Yes.*
> *Clerk.* Who shall say for you?
> **Jury.** *Our Foreman.*
> **Clerk.** Edmond Harvey *hold up thy hand. How say you, is the prisoner guilty of the Treason whereof he stands Indicted and hath been arraigned, or not Guilty?*
> **Jury.** *Guilty—*
> **Clerk.** *Look to him Keeper.*
> **Clerk.** *What Goods and Chattels, &c.*
> **Jury.** *None to our Knowledge. The same question being asked touching Alderman* Penington, Henry Marten, Gilbert

Millington, *Alderman* Titchborne, *Col.* Roe, *Col.* Lilburne, *and* Henry Smith, *they were severally found guilty by the Jury in manner aforesaid* ... (*EIA* 256–7)

What may well have troubled the foreman of the jury was the fact that there were real differences between the eight defendants, yet the jury were being told to broadbrush them all as equally guilty. The odd way in which the clerk's standard sentence '*Look to him Keeper*' – telling the warder to take firm hold of the now-declared-guilty prisoner Edmond Harvey – is preceded by a long printed dash after the word '*Guilty*' and no full-stop, strongly suggests that the foreman had been about to say something else (it being the only occasion in the entire transcript where 'Guilty' is followed by a dash, the usual symbol for an incomplete sentence) but that the clerk prevented it by interrupting him. However, that – at any rate – was the end of this part of the men's trial.

※

The executions – and no one being tried or in the public knew when they would stop or how many there would eventually be, although the prosecutors had decided – were thus the backdrop to everything that was said and done in court over the eleven days it sat. The executions would colour everything that followed them, would operate as a dreadful warning to defendants as to the probable outcome of their own trials, although most of those who had handed themselves in to the House of Commons in June would have to wait for the extra Act of Parliament to pass. Bridgeman's closing remarks made it as clear as he could that there would indeed be such an Act: execution was only being postponed, 'suspended' until that point:

There are some of you that though the judgment of death is to
passe against you, by his Majesties grace and favour, and the
mercy under him, of the two houses of Parliament, Execution
is to be suspended until another Act of Parliament shall passe
to that purpose ... (*EIA* 279)

For, as he had earlier pronounced:

You that had a hand in the Kings death ... prepare your selves
for that death which you are to die, it is a debt which we all
owe to nature ... (*EIA* 183)

And again, when he ended the second Thursday of the trial and
acknowledged that the prisoners were in different categories,
nonetheless,

though you be in these several Classes, yet what I shall say will
concern you all, because I do not know how it may fall with
you, none of us knows how soon we may come to our deaths,
some (probably) sooner then others, all must come to it ...
(*EIA* 279)

Such judgements – and the ongoing executions – would render
even those awaiting an Act of Parliament 'dismayed', and quite
possibly 'desperate' in the full sense, too ('in despair, despairing,
hopeless'); their impending executions would operate as an effective kind of torture. Not one of those on trial in the group of six
here singled out could have ended up believing that they would
not – in the end – be executed. Still, where there was life ...

6

'My last and onely Love'

The prisoners now back in the Tower were, however, in a new state. They had been condemned – attainted – for high treason, and this had had an immediate and permanent effect on their financial situations. They were to be stripped of their possessions and all their sources of income removed. We happen to know the figures in Marten's case, and exactly what that meant, following his 'attainder'. The 'Whole annual value' of his unsold estate was

> about 1000*l*.; of which 400*l*. for his wife's jointure, made before marriage, above 20 years since, out of which 2000*l*. are to be raised for portions for his two eldest daughters; 300*l*. per an. for the jointure of George Marten's wife, which is only Henry Marten's so long as he has issue male, he having now only one son ...

All that does not sound too bad – it apparently left Marten £300 a year – until the rest of the statement comes:

> There is in judgments, statutes, and mortgages upon the said 1,000*l*. per an. about 30,000*l*.; and the creditors desire to purchase from the King the reversion of the remainder although the encumbrances are about 15,000*l*. more than the whole estate can be sold for.[1]

This meant that his accumulated debts had grown to be worth not just far more than his income (£1,000) but also double what his estates were worth (£15,000). Those who had loaned him money or who had taken over his estates for their own profit now stood to lose everything, just as he had lost everything. He was for the future entirely dependent upon what his family could provide for him.

He was also, like the other prisoners similarly stripped of their income, able to do nothing except wait for the Act of Parliament, which they knew would one day come and which would end their lives. Rumours from the Commons almost immediately started to filter through to them; many of them had once been MPs, and they had relations and friends still in parliament. News of what was happening must frequently have been acquired and as quickly shared around the Tower.

As early as November 1660, in fact, the first rumours came. On 9 November the Commons walked together to the Banqueting House to hear an address from the king, and the following day one MP reported the gossip he had heard: ''Tis said Sir Hen. Martin, Tichburne, August: Garland, and Hewlet will all four be hanged.'[2] It may appear an odd grouping, but Marten (pointedly declared unrepentant by Bridgeman) and Robert Titchborne (singled out on 15 May 1660 as one 'designed to suffer in this business without mercy'[3]) were obvious targets. Garland was not only a lawyer who had helped determine procedure before the king's trial in 1649 but was accused of having spat in the king's face at the trial itself (an accusation he denied, but it would have been remembered), and Hewlet had very nearly suffered execution at the end of the trial at the Old Bailey. Another letter, two days later, declared the reports to be 'without ground'[4] that any more of the king's judges were to die, but rumours continued to circulate. On 13 November, for example, 'It was expected yesterday that Titchbourne, Henry Martin, Owen Ro, and Lilbourne, should have been executed,' and another report, of 20 November, stated that not just the selected four would be condemned but that 'the rest of the King's judges' would also be.[5]

By December 1660 it actually seemed likely to be very soon. On 8 December one MP wrote to a friend to say: 'I hear all the prisoners that stand condemned and are in the Tower are to suffer.'[6] That was his response to what had happened in the Commons the day before. The House had been engaged in the third reading of a Bill condemning to death the regicides who had fled abroad (and depriving them of their estates) – when there had been a sudden attempt to use that Bill against the prisoners in the Tower as well:

Mr. *Prynne*, upon the reading of it, observed, upon the Providence of God, That the Bill should be brought in at the very Time, which was upon the same Day twelve Years, that the King's Trial was agreed on. He therefore moved that some others of the Regicides, who had surrendered themselves, should be put into this Bill and now executed, particularly the Lawyers, and named *Garland*. Captain *Titus* seconded this Motion, and named Sir *Hardress Waller*, who, he said, was a Pensioner to the late King, saying, The *Turks* would not eat the Bread of any Man they meant to betray; and that a *Roman* Servant, who betrayed his Master, tho' for the public Good, was executed ...[7]

So the Puritan William Prynne – from Edmund Ludlow's point of view, 'desirous to ruine as many as possible of those who had bin faithfull to the publique' (meaning the people of England during the Commonwealth), and being also what Ludlow derided as a 'beauteffeu' ('boutefeu',[8] an inciter of quarrels) – had his motion seconded. The reference to 'the Providence of God' and the date was typical. He was actually wrong about the date: it was not until 28–29 December 1648 that the Commons had voted that the king should be tried. But Prynne was remembering 6–7 December 1648 and the events of Pride's Purge, when he – and many other members – had been forcibly excluded from the Commons. For him that had been the decisive move towards a (purged) Commons being prepared to put the king on trial, and he had not forgotten it. In parliament Prynne was regarded as a martyr to tyranny: in the 1630s he had had his ears cut off and his cheeks branded for offences against the Archbishop of Canterbury, William Laud, against whom he had, in turn, pursued a campaign that had ended in Laud's execution in 1645. Back in 1649 Marten had been extremely rude about Prynne, calling him 'the Crop-Eared Lawyer' and describing his tumultuous writing as 'stuft with non-sence'; he had also been very funny about Prynne's tendency to disagree with everybody ('Should the Apostles come from Heaven, sent thence to institute a Government, Mr. *Prynne* would dissent from, and wrangle with them'[9]). None of that was now going to help his chances.

But for the moment nothing came of Prynne's attempt, and parliament was dissolved on 29 December 1660 for more than four months. The great event before the next session was the king's coronation on 23 April 1661; the coronation dinner, after the ceremony in Westminster Abbey, would – as usual – be held in Westminster Hall, the first such event there since the trial of Charles I. The same system of extra scaffolds and hangings was employed as had been used at the trial (Pepys noted '10000 people … Into the hall I got – where it was very fine with hangings and scaffolds, one upon another, full of brave ladies'[10]). Illustration 13 shows how the hall would be used in an identical manner for the dinner after the coronation of James II on 23 April 1685, exactly twenty-four years later, and can be compared with Illustration 2 (see page xvii).

In May 1661, however, as soon as parliament was reassembled,

Illustration 13: 'A Prospect of the Inside of
Westminster Hall': engraving, 1685

rumours about the regicides started again. 'Some Bills are preparing for indemnity ...'[11] – indicating that there would be a new
listing of those granted indemnity, so that those excluded could
now be lined up for execution. It continued to be a nervous time.
A messenger came very late to Mary Ward's lodgings one night
and scared her. Marten wrote to her the next day:

> How did my poor Dear sleep last night, after the alarm thy man
> gave thee from hence? but thou hast been used to such things ...
> *I* shall now give some comfort to thy little heart, having lately
> perused the Kings Speech and the Chancelors, either *I* am very
> much mistaken in them, or they signifie no great danger to us,
> whose faults are almost as old as our selves. (*L* 26)

The lord chancellor, Edward Hyde, had referred to the regicides in a speech to the House of Lords on 8 May 1661: 'there will remain so few who do not deserve to be forgiven by us, that we may very well submit to the King's Advice, and His Example ...' That sounded very hopeful; if the king were prepared to set an example in magnanimously accepting the regicides' continuing existence, so, surely, should everyone else.

But rumours persisted. One of Marten's brothers-in-law, Sir George Stonhouse, who had been in the House of Commons between 1640 and 1644, was there again between 1660 and 1675, and – according to Marten in a letter to Mary Ward written on Monday, 8 July – during the previous week Stonhouse had told Marten's son Hal that

> nothing at all has been done in the house against us since one single motion on Munday was sevennight [Monday a week ago], seconded by no body. (*L* 80)

This, for Marten, was surprising, being 'contrary to what *I* had heard' (his own sources doubtless being other prisoners). But Stonhouse was in a way right. On Monday, 1 July 1661, it had been agreed (not seconded but no one against it either) that a clause should be added to a Bill primarily designed to deal with the acquisition of the estates of escaped regicides. It was thus

> *Resolved*, That the said Bill shall, according to the former Vote, contain a Clause for the Execution of those Nineteen Traitors in the *Tower*, that are convicted and condemned: And Sir *Heneage Finch*, his Majesty's Solicitor General is desired to prepare and bring in the said Bill.

This is what Prynne and others had pressed for back in November 1660, and they had clearly now won the argument. So that was that. A Bill with a clause in it confirming the death sentence was resolved on and would shortly be prepared.

It was in this situation that Marten wrote one of his most remarkable letters to Mary Ward. He had heard what had happened – but, not for the first time, the worse the news, the better he was at dealing with it. He started off:

> My last and onely Love, though I were sure to live an hundred years longer, and thou not half so many hours ...

A hundred days would be an achievement in this situation – but he loved her for ever and ever, no matter what happened. Was the news bad? Very well then:

> As for news, it cannot be worth the gaping after (any more then the weather) the worst will come soone enough; the best is like to be welcome whensoever it comes. I confess what I hear is not very good, but (just like weather again) it may rain two or three dayes in a weeke, and that in summer, and it may hold up a fortnight together, and that in the midst of winter. The Skill is, not in being weather-wise, but weather-proof.

That was the answer, to be weather-proof against the worst of news, against the threats of death. The secret is to be 'snugg like a snaile within our own selves, that is, our mindes, which nobody but we can touch' (*L* 6).

But having delivered these rather touching pieces of advice Marten characteristically admitted that it was all just words, even though he did words so well: 'I could stuff my whole sheet of paper with this discourse, but that I have a bigger providing for thee' (*L* 6), that is, I have other things to say and perhaps to send. Such a return to normality is endearing.

And anyway, as Stonhouse had effectively communicated,

nothing had actually happened. For four days in the Commons there were no developments, and then Finch was reminded of his responsibilities (some principled hardliner like Prynne must have been pushing hard). On Thursday, 4 July:

> *Ordered*, That Mr. Solicitor General do bring in a Bill, To-morrow Morning, for Execution of the Persons, Prisoners in the *Tower*, condemned for the horrid Murder of his late Sacred Majesty King *Charles* the First.

But even then nothing happened. Finch may have wanted time to get it right, while the Commons – conscious of the end of the session approaching – was also having to get through a great deal of other business. At all events, the Bill about the regicides did not come up again in the current session of parliament, the session ending on 30 July 1661.

But Marten – when reassuring Mary on Saturday, 6 July that indeed nothing had happened – went on to explain what he had been told (presumably by another prisoner, who would have heard it from someone else again):

> Sir H[eneage]. F[inch]. coming to the king to excuse himselfe for not bringing in the bills yesterday according to order, was told by his Majesty himself, he should be at no further trouble about that business, for he intended to pardon them all ... (*L* 46–7)

But this news was simply hearsay, its source unknown; there was nothing there that could be trusted. It may indeed simply have been that someone was aware of Finch's failure to produce the promised Bill and clause and had drawn the hopeful conclusion that the king must have told him not to bother. From what we know of the attitude of the king towards the regicides, that is unlikely; and Marten, not wishing to trust the rumour, asked Mary to go to hear the sermon preached before the king on Sunday 7th, as 'without question, as White-hall pipes, Westminster will dance' (L 46), meaning that the House of Commons would follow the lead given by the court.

So Stonhouse might have been right in his optimism that nothing would happen, but the matter of the executions was simply being postponed. It may even start to look as if the parliamentary body Marten had referred to back in the late summer of 1660 as 'our old enraged and new empowred enemies' (L 1) was now deliberately drawing things out as a kind of torture for those imprisoned … but it seems a good deal more likely that in July other matters had truly been more important to Finch.

However, as a way of reminding the regicides in the Tower and their families that they had not been forgotten, on 8 July 1661 the House of Commons not only set in motion the confiscation of the estates of all deceased regicides – something that had already been done to all surviving regicides – but to assure the prisoners in the Tower of its power of life and death over them, the Commons also set down an order that

> those now in Custody … should all be drawn upon Sledges with Ropes about their Necks, from the Tower of London to, and under the Gallows at Tyburn, and thence convey'd back to the Tower, there to remain Prisoners during their Lives.

This painful and humiliating ceremony was to be 'solemnly executed' on 'the 30th January following', the anniversary of the execution of Charles I. The regicides were being reminded of exactly what the Commons would be doing when it eventually passed the promised Bill – condemning them to execution for high treason with all the ceremony of hanging, drawing, and quartering involved.

A prisoner on the way to be hanged would usually be taken tied up in a cart, the cart driven under the gallows, the neck of the prisoner secured in a ready-prepared noose, the ropes tying him to the cart removed, the clergyman present offering some prayers, the prisoner making a final speech. And then the cart would drive on. But prisoners convicted of treason or high treason were sent on a humiliating and painful journey to Tyburn lashed to hurdles drawn by horses. They would pass first along the public streets and then out on roads towards Tyburn. They had to be secured; period images suggest that they were tied sitting or lying, either singly or in pairs. They would have been helpless to avoid any pelting with old fruit or rotten eggs (or anything more disgusting that came to hand) or being targets for stones or dogs chasing them along the journey. It was five miles to Tyburn; they would have been two to three hours on the road there, and the same would have been needed to get them back, after a pause at Tyburn under the permanent three-sided structure of the gallows. They would have been black and blue with bruises afterwards, from the banging and jolting over cobbles, stones, and ruts, and filthy with mud and dust (if tied lying down, heads towards the horses' tails, falling horse dung in the face would have been another near certainty).

However, there was an interesting side-effect to the Commons' decision. It meant that the regicides in the Tower could expect still to be alive on 30 January 1662. This was odd; it seems possible that those in the Commons who would have preferred the regicides to 'remain Prisoners during their Lives' were attempting – by initiating such a commemorative ceremony – to propitiate those in parliament (William Prynne, for example) who would have preferred the regicides to be executed immediately. But although the regicides probably felt safe for a while, they nevertheless must have known that they were getting close to the end of any possible further delays; the 'Lives' during which they would 'remain Prisoners' would not be long ones.

※

Mary Ward and Marten had once hoped that Mary and the children would leave for Derbyshire to live at a farmhouse Marten had owned, now in the hands of his Derbyshire agent Richard Peters – the journey planned for autumn, probably September – with Marten hoping to see Mary as often as possible before she went. Back at the time before Marten had been committed to the Tower and his estates seized, Mary had hoped to buy a coach for the journey with the children, although Marten had counselled her to hire one. Whatever means of travel they were now considering, winter would not be a good time, autumn far preferable – 'the weather and ways too are very tolerable yet', Marten had told her, probably around October 1660 or 1661, 'and it is a huge while to maintain a family in *Hockney* lodgings till the Spring' (*L* 13). Hackney – a large, well-to-do village of 260 houses on the Roman Road running north-east out of London – was convenient for messengers to and from the Tower, although not the cheapest of places to live.

But, as money grew tighter, the planned mode of transport to Derbyshire was reduced to horseback; Marten's agent Peters had sent his servant Robin up to London on a horse, and it even seemed possible to Mary that 'one or two horses and a paire of panniers' (*L* 27) might carry her and the children back to Derbyshire (the children in the pannier baskets). But then Marten had to send Robin back at short notice, thus losing a servant and the horse he came on – and that for the moment was the end of what Marten termed Mary's 'pitifull pannier-plot' (*L* 74), which does indeed sound pretty makeshift. The trip was postponed; and the later it was planned for, the less likely it is that it ever took place.

Because things were starting to go badly wrong for them both. There was nothing as alarming as when Henryetta (Bacon-hog) had been born, when it had seemed possible that she would not survive: 'my poor skin-and-bone brat' (L 34) Marten had called her.[12] But even when in prison Marten wrote anxiously to the mother with a sickly baby on her lap: 'My little baby does not lie upon my lap, but she lies almost as heavie as if she did, till *I* hear how she is' (L 38). He was, though, as worried about Mary's state as he was about the baby's:

> *My poor sweet soul,*
> That I could send thee my two armes and hands at the ends of 'um enclosed in a Letter: for indeed I begin now to be as much afraid of thee as of my little baby, and of the two I know which would be most missed, to say nothing of the simple thing called love ... Prethee Dear, think of some body to help thee in this luggage. (L 24)

'Luggage' signified precisely 'what has to be lugged about', as the baby had to be. But Marten very much wanted to see the baby. When Mary was visiting him he hoped she could 'bring my sick baby at least with thee' (L 64). Later he heard 'how fine and well my little brat came on', although he remained cautious, she felt so small and vulnerable: 'such worms are set up with a rush [set upright with a stalk], and thrown down again with a straw' (L 63). And then, while teething, she acquired her Bacon-hog nickname from getting raw meat into her mouth, and she also had trouble with her toes, 'poore Bacon-hog ... with her little toosses' (L 18).

There is evidence in Marten's letters that Mary was in desperate trouble, being pursued by creditors, and some time in the summer of 1661 he started to fear that they had actually lost touch because she had been arrested for debt. But he was not sure even of that; all he could do was beg her to tell him.

Love, if thou beest in any prison, or bayliffs house, or such ugly place, doe not hide it from me, as thou wouldst (and as I would have thee) from *Peggie* and *Sarah*. I can bear it, and perhaps advise thee to bear it, and perhaps what to do in it before the Judges of the Kings Bench be gone out of town, and before thou hast gotten that (with being stifled up this hot weather) which thou wilt not claw off again in hast. (*L* 56)

For those 'stifled up' in the King's Bench Prison there was an ever-present danger of disease; Marten wanted Mary out of prison (if she was *in* prison) before the end of the legal year at the end of July, when the judges left for the country and those in prison had no chance of getting out before the autumn.

What made it worse for him was that Mary – wherever she was – had been seen by other people who *did* know where she was: a messenger called Stephen who visited Marten (and who might even have been carrying this actual letter back to her) told Marten that Mary's brother Job was visiting her – 'and why,' Marten protested to her, 'I might not have been as well of thy counsel as he (if it were not as I suspect) I doe not understand'. He obviously thought she must have been arrested. Even more strangely to Marten, their customary messenger Dick Pettingall was available 'and needed no letter to trust with it' – he could just have brought the news. Nevertheless,

if there be no remedy but thou must be kept from thy little ones, I will try all the strength I have to get one or two of them hither to me, and the third nearer to thee, that house-keeping may be struck off at Kennington, and the bantlings finde more comfort then now they can at such distance from both their parents. (*L* 56)

He was baffled that she had not told him what had happened, and he remained helplessly worried about the children.

If she *had* been arrested for debt it was probably not for the first time. Marten had advised her what to do if approached by an official such as a bailiff, one of 'the Kites and Jack-daws in breeches or long coats' for whom – after long experience – he cared 'not a figg' (*L* 57). She had previously just escaped arrest:

> My poor sweet Dear, what *I* have been afraid of a great while, and thou hast just scaped so narrowly, is more likely then ever to fall upon thee, because the whole tribe of Bayliffs and Catch-poles will be exasperated against thee, and have thee by hook or by crook; and it is a huge disadvantage to have the *Law* of the land for an enemy. (*L* 54)

A catchpole was a petty warrant officer who arrested those in debt, as Marten would have known. Mary had possessions in store, and Marten had helped her move them while he was himself out of prison, probably late in 1659. But although, as he said, '*I* will try all the wayes *I* can above ground to help thee', all the same,

> if an officer come that thou thinkest is one indeed, thou must give him thy right name; thou maist tell him thy other too, and bid him set down both, for thou art known and called by both. (*L* 7)

She was both Mary Ward and Mary Marten.

But in that same letter were signs of the strain they were both under. For once Marten had absolutely nothing to send her – he could not even pay the girl who was taking his letter for him ('*I* have not a penny to give her'), let alone pass on any money to Mary: 'I have nothing to enclose in my paper, but the same heart which was thine before' (*L* 7). If things were to continue like that – even after the Monday when he should get his allowance – it would not have been surprising if they had started to drift apart. Another letter from Marten began: '*My Dear*, It is a filthy long while since we either saw or heard from one another, yet don't let's chide, for I think verily it is no wilfull fault in either of us.' And, just as ever, he wanted to know 'how all my 3 pocky rogues do? and tell me true too' (*L* 61). It must have felt a very long time since the relatively happy days towards the end of 1659 when he was able to tell her that '*I* long to have thee with me for good and all, and sometimes I fancy it not altogether impossible,' and when he could even fantasise about being rich one day. He had then been writing to her from his lodgings, not from prison, and commenting on the way

that winter is a more chargeable season then summer, especially when two chimneys are to be warmed instead of one, and parlours call for candles as well as chambers. Now I talke like a miserable cribbe [miser], because *I* would put thee in hopes that *I* may be a rich man yet before I die; and then I warrant thou wilt love,

   My Heart,

      Thy owne,

         H. Marten. (*L* 34)

Those had been the days when he could send a bearer to Mary with instructions for shopping in Southwark Market: '3s. 6d. for a joynt of meat at his discretion, 1 s. for a loaf of bread, and 2 s. for a quart bottle of Canary, and 1 s. for himself' (*L* 24). *That* kind of money – 7s. 6d. for a single round of purchases – was a sign of how well off Marten and Mary had once been.

But it becomes horribly clear in some letters that can be dated late in the sequence (probably in the second half of 1661) that not

only Marten's financial resources but – with them – his ability
to remain Mary Ward's 'Dear' were drying up. The phrase 'a
kept mistress' dates from the period,[13] and Marten could, quite
simply, no longer afford to keep Mary. By November 1661 things
were seriously worsening. The following is the opening of what
is probably one of his last surviving letters to her:

> *My poor sweet Dear,*
> Would I could do thee halfe so much good as thou dost me
> in letting me know how thou dost, though it be far otherwise
> then I would have thee. *Tom Peyton* told me indeed that thou
> took'st a vomit last Sunday, but wert pretty well upon it. *I*
> am afraid *I* can guesse too right at the greatest part of thy
> disease, or at least, the ground of it, which is melancholy
> and thoughtfulness for things, which *I* can apply no remedy
> to ... (*L* 10)

What had made things far worse for him was the fact that
both Major John Wildman and John Loder – on whom he had
been relying to pass on income from the land Marten had sold
them – could no longer supply him. By the end of November
1661 Wildman had been committed to prison and Loder had
had some kind of 'restraint' put on him. Marten could now
hardly afford to send letters to Mary: he was glad 'when thou
dost furnish me with messengers, partly to save the charge of
a porter, and chiefly to understand how it is with thee and my
children' (*L* 10).

But to her – and from what we know of him, to himself, too
– he remained determinedly optimistic; he had always 'found a
twig or something to hold me up'. For the moment he simply
had to use any large sum of money he acquired to pay his bills
at the Tower:

I am resolved that the next 30. l. which comes shall be the Lieu-
tenants; lesser summes may do the rest of thy body service;
But that must cure thy heart, which dwells here with
   My Soul, thy true
     H. Marten. (*L* 10)

❉

But by 1661 he also knew – and Mary knew – that he would not
be able to do much to support her in the future. Once in the past
– perhaps back in 1658 or 1659 – she had written to tell him that
she had had an offer 'of a new Dear', and even then he could
have done nothing except advise her to accept. She had asked
him to burn her letter:

> Though I burnt thy Letter so soon as *I* had read it, according
> to thy order by the bearer, yet *I* have not forgotten the contents
> of it. Concerning the offer thou hast of a new Dear, there was
> a time *I* confesse, when I was such a Hog, as to think my throat
> cut by any body that would have a share in thee besides my
> self: *I* am reformed, but not the ordinary way, by not caring
> who enjoyes that which I have done taking pleasure in, but by
> binding up all my pleasure in thine: and as it has been pretty
> common with me to think that good bit tasted best which
> went into thy mouth; so still or more do I relish thy happinesse
> beyond my own ... (*L* 37)

He had *not* 'done taking pleasure' in her; despite everything he
writes an intensely sensually reminiscent letter (shown by the
word 'relish', the repeated 'pleasure' and by the memory of the
'good bit' which 'tasted best'). But all he could do was to tell
her – if she wanted to satisfy *him* (and he had no doubt that she
did) – then she had to 'study how to satisfie thy own mind'; that

is, do what *she* thought was best with such an offer of 'a new Dear'. There was just one hint ('an item') he wanted to give her:

> For all that, *I* cannot let thee goe without an item. My poor Heart, take heed of every body, especially of the fairest offers; thou hast been bitten, and bitten, and bitten by such as were no meer strangers to thee; by that time thou art a little older thou wilt take every word thou hearest for an errand [arrant] lie, the world is grown so false. (*L* 37)

To be 'bitten' is to be deceived; she had had a bad time in the past and was likely not to believe even the good things she heard. He insisted that she was still his 'poor Heart' (although 'poor' has a double meaning), but for the moment, though, all he could do was simply desire to see the children – and ideally her, too, although he had to put her second because seeing the children was easier in every way. Someone could bring them:

> My brats will dine with me, and Harry C— brings them. *I* would fain have them neer me, and thee too, if possible. I rest.
>   My Dearest
>   Thy everlasting self,
>   *H. M.* (*L* 37)

So he offers himself as everlastingly hers, even though he knows he is in a wretchedly dangerous situation and fears it might be the end of their relationship. Although he loves her he must be prepared to 'let thee goe', perfectly exemplifying Graham Swift's maxim: 'To love is to be ready to lose, it's not to have, to keep.'[14]

It seems just possible that since Marten had been in the Tower Mary had embarked on some kind of relationship with no less a person than Sir John Robinson. Marten on one occasion wrote to her: '*I* am not jealous of thy extraordinary kindness to our

Lievtenant, but am content to be as kind as thou art, if I had wherewithall' (*L 62*) – that is, the 'means to do so' – and she, after all, had the means to attract a man that he simply did not possess. Whether Robinson – a married man since 1654 but born in 1615, so thirteen years younger than Marten – really might have been a 'new Dear' or had simply been flirtatious, we have no way of knowing. But in 1661 or 1662 Mary was unlikely to have turned down the offer of a 'new Dear' as she had apparently once done. Following August 1662 Marten was sent to prison after prison, all around England, and there was no way in which Mary Ward could have followed him. (It is, however, also remotely possible that Robinson – if he had really developed a relationship with Mary – would have had reason to want Marten out of London.)

※

After the end of the parliamentary session in July 1661, and another four-month prorogation during which parliament did not sit, both Houses started new sessions on Wednesday, 20 November. Solicitor general Heneage Finch had been busy in the intervening period. The Bill promised in July was given the brief but ruthlessly clear title 'Executing Regicides' in the *Journal of the House of Commons*, and within two days of the start of the new session it had had its formal first reading, on Friday, 22 November 1661. Yet another beginning of an end. On 16 October 1660 Orlando Bridgeman had declared that 'Execution is to be suspended untill another Act of Parliament shall pass to that purpose' (*EIA 279*). Now, thirteen months later, parliament had the 'Bill for executing certain Persons which are attainted for High Treason' in front of it. Execution was to be suspended no longer.

7

Commons

It must have been agreed that the Bill 'Executing Regicides' would be given priority in the Commons. There were factions at work impatient with the continued existence of the regicides, and concerned families and friends could presumably implement no further delays. Following the formal first reading of the new Bill, the second reading was timetabled for Monday, 25 November, when a large attendance was not just desired but expected: '*Resolved*, upon the Question, That this Bill be read again the Second time on *Monday* Morning next, at Ten of the Clock, when the House is full.'

But not only would the Bill be read the Commons had decided to operate, in effect, as the penultimate stage of a criminal process, and those accused were being offered a final chance to plead for their lives:

> And that such of the Persons attainted, named in the Bill, as are now in the *Tower*, do then appear, and have Liberty to offer what they can for themselves. And Sir *John Robinson*, Lieutenant of the *Tower*, is to give Notice hereof to the Persons before-mentioned; and to cause them to be brought on *Monday*, at Ten of the Clock, to attend this House.

So, on Monday, 25 November, the twelve prisoners in the Tower (ten of them had been MPs themselves at some point) would be brought in turn to the bar of the House of Commons to say 'what they can for themselves'. Another miniature trial, with the prisoners pleading at the bar, was thus set up.

Marten and the others were told about it by Robinson by Sunday, 24 November at the latest, for that day Marten wrote to Mary Ward one of his two letters to her that can be dated with absolute security:

> *My dearest Dear,*
> Thou hast *I* hope by this time digested one shrewd brunt, and art the better prepared for another. To morrow morning we are all to appear at the House of Commons, to shew cause why the sentence given against us should not be executed. I think we can shew a very good one, wherein the Kings honour and the Paliaments [*sic*] is concerned: if they think otherwise, who can help it? That can
> My sweet Love,
> Thy own for ever
> and ever,   *H. Marten. (L* 19)

The 'one shrewd brunt' (jarring shock) she had already digested may have had nothing to do with the proceedings of the Commons but may have been some move against her for debt. All the same, Marten would have been very conscious, when he wrote the words 'Thy own for ever / and ever', how near he was to writing a last letter, which gives a special poignancy to the way he is hers 'for ever / and ever'. His belief that the prisoners have a 'very good' argument is one he would like her to believe, but the sudden demand made on the prisoners for further self-defence was certainly another 'shrewd brunt'.

On the Monday the prisoners were brought to the Commons:

Owen Roe, Henry Smith, Robert Tichburne, James Temple,

Wm. Havingham, Gilbert Millington, Augustine Garland, Henry Martin, George Fleetwood, Thomas Waite, Peter Temple, and *John Downes*, Twelve of the said Persons attainted of High Treason, being in the Custody of the Lieutenant of the *Tower*, were successively brought to the Bar by the Serjeant attending this House.

Their argument – as summarised in the proceedings of the Commons – was that, according to

His Majesty's gracious Declaration from *Breda*, and the Votes of this House, and his Majesty's Proclamation of the Sixth of *June* in the Twelfth Year of his Reign, published by Advice of the Lords and Commons then assembled, they did render themselves, being advised that they should thereby secure their Lives; and humbly craved the Benefit thereof, and the Mercy of this House, and their Mediation to his Majesty, on their Behalves.

The only evidence of what was actually said, however, besides that general solemn plea, survives in the *Journal of the House of Commons*; and relates to only one individual:

Harry Marten briskly added, That he had never obey'd any Proclamation before this, and hoped that he should not be hang'd for taking of the King's word now.

His liveliness (in the old sense of 'brisk') was not just responsible for a good joke but sent it on its way into the popular imagination. Just a year later James Heath would quote it in his (wretchedly inaccurate) chronicle of recent years:

On the 25 of the same Month [November 1661] the Regicides ... were brought to the barre of the house of Lords, to answer what they could for themselves why judgement should not be executed ... *Henry Marten* added that he never obeyed any Proclamation before but this and hoped that he should not be hanged for taking the Kings word now ...[1]

And in 1665 the violently royalist commentator William Winstanley repeated it, along with the mistake 'Lords' for 'Commons' (typically copying from Heath without acknowledgement):

being brought to the Bar of the House of Lords to Answer why Judgement should not be Executed upon him, he replyed, That he understood the Proclamation extended to favour of life upon rendering himself; and withall added, That he never obeyed any of his Majesties Proclamations before but this, and hoped that he should not be Hanged for taking the Kings Word now ...

Winstanley hated Marten and happily extended Heath's description of him as 'a most leud, vicious and infamous person' into 'a most Wicked, Lewd, Vicious; and Infamous Person, whose Actions have rendered him odious to all Posterity'.[2] He may have cited the quip to show how little respect Marten had for the king, but it comes across, all the same, as wonderfully spirited and suggests that even Winstanley may, in spite of himself, have been impressed.

The fact is that the signatories of the king's death warrant had apparently done everything required of them and had trusted themselves to 'the King's word'. Was the House of Commons now going to ignore or overrule 'the King's word'? What Marten says constitutes his way of reminding the House of Commons, wittily but also very firmly, that what it was preparing to do arguably ran counter to the king's intention in that famous original statement issued at Breda:

we do grant a full and generall Pardon, which we are ready to
pass under our great Seal of England, to all our Subjects of
what degree or quality soever, who within fourty dayes after
the publication hereof shall lay hold upon this our grace and
favour, and shall by any publick Act declare their doing so;
And that they return to the Loyalty and Obedience of good
Subjects ...

Those were undeniably the words of the king published on
14 April, however much he might have been swayed – or have
changed his mind – since. 'Our Proclamation' of 6 June had actually been written by the Commons for the king to pronounce:

That all and every the Persons before named shall, within
Fourteen Days next after the Publishing of this Our Royal
Proclamation, personally appear and render themselves to the
Speaker or Speakers of Our House of Peers and Commons, or
unto the Lord Mayor of Our City of *London*, or to the Sher-
iffs of Our respective Counties of *England* and *Wales*, under
Pain of being excepted from any Pardon or Indemnity both for
their respective Lives and Estates.

And Marten and the others could argue that they had indeed
rendered themselves, to qualify for 'Pardon or Indemnity'.

On Tuesday 26th the Commons met again and had 'a long
Debate' on the Bill in front of them, in the course of which
the Proclamation of 6 June 1660 was actually read aloud for
the assembled members to decide whether the prisoners could
indeed be right to trust to it.

And it was not to be trusted; nor could the prisoners rely upon
the Declaration of Breda of May 1660, for it would immediately have become apparent that Marten (and the others) were
attempting to ignore what was included in the Declaration of

Breda after its comments on 'the Loyalty and Obedience of good Subjects', and following the ellipsis that closes the quotation above:

> … excepting only such Persons as shall hereafter be excepted by Parliament, Those only excepted.

So parliament had always had the right to except the people it chose from the king's pardon. That is what it had done in the summer of 1660 and that was exactly what it was proposing to do in November 1661.

Then came the vote, which took the form of a motion not to proceed with the Bill:

> The Question being put, That, upon Consideration of the King's Majesty's Proclamation, pleaded by the Prisoners brought Yesterday to the Bar, the Bill for their Execution should be laid aside. The House was divided …

But, in the language of parliament, 'the Noes went forth', winning with a surprisingly comfortable majority of 124 to 109. And so, in the abstruse terminology of the Commons, 'it passed in the Negative'. The House had rejected the attempt to lay aside the Bill; it was going forward to its committee stage.

That was on Tuesday, 26 November. By that night Marten was aware of what had happened. We do not know his source, but it may have been Stonhouse. The news occasioned one of the most striking of his letters, a candidate indeed for any collection of loving letters. He sent it to Mary Ward around the Thursday of that week, and it shows how he could write *in extremis*, because this really did seem to be the end of the road. She had to be both brave and gallant to cope with it:

I was told on Tuesday night, that the House of Commons had given us all up on monday, and had appointed a Committee to bring in a bill for that purpose, which cannot require much time ... (*L* 66)

All he could offer her were 'such cordials as ordinary people give to one another' – cordials being not just alcohol, but things 'to invigorate the heart'; he had a list of them:

Perhaps the bill will not pass when it comes in, perhaps the Lords will not passe it, when it comes there; perhaps the King has given way to his friends to set this on foot, on purpose to have the whole honour of pardoning to himself; perhaps some names may be excepted in one House, or in the other; and thy Deare may be one of them. (*L* 66)

He would have preferred not to have passed on the news, 'but that *I* was afraid thou wouldst hear it from another hand, that would make it worse'. Instead, he offered the kind of comradeship that was its own kind of intense, still-smiling consolation. '*My sweet Dear, brave gallant Soul,* Now stand thy ground ... Pluck up thy strength, my good Heart, conquer this brunt, and thou art a man for ever' (*L* 66). It's a kind of tender jesting in a terrible situation, and quite remarkable.

And, crucially, there were the children: 'Look upon my little brats, and see if thy Deare be not among them; has not one of 'um his face, another his braines, another his mirth?' (*L* 66). There was nothing else on which she could still count, after years in which they had both lost so much – their property, their possessions, their money, their chance of living together – and with Marten now in extreme danger of losing his life. What she had to do was simply to look at the children, for it is just the best thing in this world, and a thing that could not be taken from me, when Lemster [Leominster] was, when all the remainder of my Estate and thine was; nor when my liberty and the assurance of my life was, nor when thy company was, which though *I* reckon last, goes for something with

    My dearest Dear,
      Thy own,
        H. Marten. (L 66–7)

It is a letter to bring a lump into the throat, not in spite of but because of the spirit and tenderness still operating in it, as in the lovely mock-diffidence of the way her 'company' – still with an intimate, sexual sense in the mid-seventeenth century – 'goes for something with ... Thy own', which he still is, as she is 'My dearest Dear'.

※

The House of Commons had indeed given Marten up; it had played its part in ensuring that he would be executed. But there was (for once, literally) a stay of execution. The Commons does not just wave such a Bill through. As Marten knew, it puts it in front of a committee – and this one seems to have taken all the time it could, as its very make-up might suggest. I quote the entry in full (except for four repeated names, where I have removed the repetitions), although I invite the reader – first – simply to note the names of William Prynne and Sir John Robinson, no friends to Marten, but also that of John Lovelace, son of Marten's brother-in-law, and second, to observe the number of strongly royalist members. Sir Maurice Berkeley (who had been rewarded with a baronetcy in July 1660 for taking the news of Monck's declaration in favour of restoration across to the exiled court of Charles II in Holland), for example, Henry Cavendish (Lord Mansfield, who had presented himself to Charles II at Dover in 1660 and had been rewarded with the mastership of the robes), Sir Humphrey Winch (also awarded a baronetcy in June 1660), and Sir Solomon Swale (who had suffered severely for his loyalty during the parliamentary war and had been presented with the first baronetcy conferred after the Restoration). These were not individuals to have any sympathy with regicides.

Resolved, upon the Question, That the said Bill, for Execution of the Persons attainted of High Treason, be committed to Mr. Lovelace, Mr. Vaughan, Sir Henry North, Sir Maurice Berkeley, Sir Courtney Poole, Mr. Bulkley, Sir George Ryve, Mr. Dowdswell, Sir Edward Wise, Mr. Reymes, Mr. Higgons, Mr. Pryn, Mr. Devereux, Lord Cornebury, Sir John Covert, Mr. Thurland, Mr. Fane, Sir Henry Worsley, Mr. Knight, Mr. Peckham, Sir Baynham Throckmorton, Mr. Tomkins, Colonel Legg, Sir Edm. Peirse, Colonel Gilby, Sir Charles Harbord, Sir Edward Vaughan, Mr. Birch, Mr. Potter, Mr. Clarke, Mr. Jones, Serjeant Charleton, Serj. Keeling, Sir Phillip Warwicke, Lord Newburgh, Sir John Goodricke, Mr. Goodricke, Sir Edmond Bowyer, Mr. Clifford, Mr. Churchill, Sir Solomon Swale, Mr. Swinfein, Sir John Shaw, Mr. Yorke, Sir John Nicholas, Sir Robert Holt, Sir Hump. Winch, Mr. Whorwood, Mr. Low, Sir Henry Puckering, Sir Tho. Strickland, Mr. Scudamore, Mr. Weld, Mr. Rigby, Mr. Attorney of the Duchy, Mr. Harbord, Mr. Mountague, Sir John Vaughan, Mr. Steward, Sir Theop. Biddolph, Sir John Robinson, Mr. Pleadwell, Sir Thomas Meeres, Sir Allan Broderick, Mr. Walrond, Sir Tho. Littleton, Sir Rich. Temple, Mr. Bulteele, Lord Mansfeild.

The committee was to meet on Wednesday 27th in the Star Chamber – the room in the Old Palace of Westminster notorious for the Court of Star Chamber, which had sat there without a jury until 1641 but which had been abolished in the first months of the Long Parliament when the Commons had managed to destroy some of the unjust institutions of arbitrary monarchical government and when Marten had first been an MP. It was now simply a convenient meeting room, where a committee preparing to send some of those same MPs to their deaths could

> take into Consideration the Petitions, Affidavits, and other Papers, tendered by the Prisoners: And to send for Papers, Persons, and Records.

As they would be sending for all those papers, there could be no immediate conclusion. The size of the committee – sixty-nine – would also have been reassuring to Marten's friends; it is far harder (and much slower) to get anything done in a large committee than in a small one. If everything has to be copied, too, for the members of the committee, that will add greatly to the time their business will take.

The committee first met on Wednesday, 27 November, but then, again, nothing appears to have happened, down to the start of the Commons' adjournment for Christmas on 20 December. It then took the rest of the Commons until Friday, 10 January – the far side of the Christmas recess – to realise that their committee was stalling and to demand action:

> *Ordered*, That the Committee to whom the Bill for Execution of certain Persons attainted of High Treason is committed, be revived; and do meet on *Tuesday* next, in the Afternoon, at Two of the Clock; and all the Members of this House, who shall come to the said Committee, are to have Votes thereat: And the Committee are desired to hasten their Report.

They even officially added another twenty-two members to the committee meeting originally planned for Tuesday 14th but, in fact, postponed to Thursday 16th, when it was again urged into revival:

> On that day, *Ordered*, That the Committee to whom the Bill for Executing certain Persons attainted of High Treason is committed, be revived: And that Mr. *Gawdy*, be added to the said Committee.

Gawdy was William Gawdy, an MP excluded in Pride's Purge who had chosen to attend Charles II at the Hague in May 1660; he had re-entered the House as an MP in 1661. A clearly royalist ninety-third member! And any other member of the Commons who chose to attend would also have a vote.

The committee's second 'revival' shook it up. The following day, Friday, 17 January, it reported what it could about the king's executioners, and finally, on the following Tuesday, 21 January, it actually got to its report stage. It had decided it wanted amendments: it wanted the names of John Downes and George Fleetwood removed from the Bill. That was accepted by the whole House. It also wanted the name of William Heveningham removed. Not accepted. It offered a petition from Henry Smith (presumably one of the 'Petitions, Affidavits, and other Papers, tendered by the Prisoners' which it had collected) to the Commons. And it was agreed that the Bill in this amended form should be 'engrossed', that is, written out in legal form, a sign that it was – for the moment – complete.

This was now a Bill for the third reading and meant that – assuming it were passed by the Lords (and there could really be not much doubt about that) – the regicides would be executed. Marten had been kept informed back in November of what was happening; he almost certainly knew about this, too. After a couple more delays – were their friends still trying to save them? – the Bill was given its third reading in the House of Commons on Saturday, 25 January and was then automatically forwarded to the House of Lords.

The timing may have been – probably was – accidental, but rumour immediately took its course. What Ludlow could reconstruct, from his particular perspective, was that

> The common reporte and expectation was that those poore lambes in the Tower who had the bloody sentence pronounced against them, and already put in execution as farr as the unnaturall and perfidious Howse of Comons could contribute thereto, should be sacrificed the same day of January that the late tyrant was executed ...[3]

So the executions would happen on 30 January. What could be more appropriate?

The prisoners in the Tower would have heard about this, and it would have linked up in their minds with the extraordinary re-enactment the Commons had specified for them back in July, of being dragged to Tyburn on hurdles on 30 January. What had been specified as a dress rehearsal for their execution must now have been perceived as the performance itself: the real thing.

In the event, the timetable slipped. It was only on 29 January 1662 that the Lords managed a first reading of the Bill for the prisoners' execution; it could not now be passed as an Act before the 30th. And it may have been made known that the Lords would also like to see the prisoners individually, just as the Commons had, so they could not be sent off to Tyburn for a whole day.

But rather than abandon the original plan of a dress rehearsal, three other victims were selected; Sir Henry Mildmay, William Monson, formerly Viscount Monson (incidentally in prison for debt in 1659, like Henry Marten), and Robert Wallop. All three had been commissioners for the king's trial in January 1649 but had neither signed the king's death warrant nor been present when the court's verdict had been pronounced and therefore had not been at the Old Bailey in October 1660 nor sentenced to death. They were, however, still in the hands of the Serjeant at Arms of the Commons, and he handed them over to Robinson, so that on Thursday 30th they could be taken through the symbolic (albeit also extremely painful) re-enactment that the Commons had planned – and the regicides would have been acutely aware of it. Very probably on the same hurdles used in October 1660, brown and black with dried blood, originally for the prisoners on their way to execution and subsequently for the baskets containing their quartered remains, as met in the street by Evelyn, the three men now in the Tower were dispatched for that horrible journey to Tyburn and back. The unaccustomed fresh air would not have compensated. But, back in the Tower, black and blue though they would have been, they would still have known themselves safer than any of the regicides. No one could have been in any doubt about what the Lords would conclude about *them*.

The Lords had throughout been the House more savagely angry with those who had killed the king. What is more, they had had a series of encounters with Henry Marten. Back in April 1643, in the Painted Chamber of the Parliament (the room where members of the two houses met), Algernon Percy, Earl of Northumberland and one of the most senior of the nobility, had accused Marten of opening a letter he had sent from Oxford, Marten suspecting that the earl had been double-dealing in his negotiations (on behalf of parliament) with the king. For this, the earl had assaulted Marten with the cane he carried. Marten had accused the earl of a breach of privilege, and the Commons had supported him by sending an official message to the Lords about it, demanding reparation; in the Lords the earl had accused

Marten of a breach of privilege in opening his letter, and the Lords had backed him,[4] but the matter had been dropped.

And then, in July 1643 it had been the Lords that had attempted to stop Marten's Commons committee from creating a new Great Seal for parliament to add authenticity to the decisions it took in the absence of the king (the unique matrix of the Great Seal was in Charles's safe-keeping in Oxford). The seal was the circular, double-sided silver matrix used to create the wax seals affixed to significant state documents and authorising, for example, all Acts of Parliament. In 1647 the seal would still be defined as the ruler's 'greatest and highest command' and as 'not controllable, nor to be dispensed with' (in 1688 King James II apparently believed that when fleeing the country he could paralyse government by throwing his Great Seal into the Thames). On 11 July 1643 the Commons had got as far as having Marten 'bring hither the Man that will undertake to grave the Great Seal, to receive his Directions'. But the House of Lords objected, as had been foreseeable, and in August 1643 Marten would be committed to the Tower and his work towards a new seal abandoned.

It would not be until 24 June 1646 that the king's Great Seal was given up on the surrender of Oxford to the Parliamentarian Army; on 11 August 1646 it would be ceremonially defaced and broken up by order of the House of Commons. It was an odd but crucial object for a dominant House of Commons to be concerned with, but possession of its own seal was a sign that the Commons *was* the new power in the land and that neither the king nor the House of Lords had any place in power.[5] Early in 1649 Marten's committee had gone ahead again, and a new Great Seal, designed by the noted engraver Thomas Simon – selected by Marten in 1643 – would be the first seal since the rule of William the Conqueror not to show the ruler holding orb and sceptre on one side and on horseback on the other, and

Illustration 14: Impression of the Great Seal of
the Commonwealth, second version

it would also be the first not to have its inscriptions in Latin but
in English.[6] Bulstrode Whitelocke, a commissioner of the seal
in the 1650s, noted that, 'This was for the most part, the fancy
of Mr. *Henry Martin* ... more particularly the inscriptions.'[7] As
so often, it was Marten who did the words, which speak for his
Leveller-inspired ideal of helping his country escape the Norman
yoke of monarchy and aristocracy.

It is hard not to conclude that Marten must also have influ-
enced Simon about what the overall design should be. There

would be a detailed map of England and Ireland on one side, representing the whole people, and on the other the sitting House of Commons with a speech being made, listened to, commented on, and discussed. The House of Lords – not just the king – was thus symbolically and very obviously passed over.

The 1648/9 version (only damaged copies survive) was inscribed 'IN THE FIRST YEARE OF FREEDOME BY GODS BLESSING RESTORED 1648'.[8] A second, slightly altered design (with the wording changed to 'THIRD YEARE'), dates from 1651, the words 'FREEDOME' and 'RESTORED' in Marten's inscription being especially interesting. When had England previously been free? According to Aubrey, Marten's claim had already been criticised by the elder Sir Henry Vane in the House of Commons over the March 1649 wording of the 'Act for the abolishing the Kingly Office in England and Ireland', whereby

> a most happy way is made for this Nation (if God see it good) *to return to its just and ancient Right* of being governed by its own Representatives ... from time to time chosen and entrusted for that purpose by the people –

How could the nation now 'return to its just and ancient Right' if such a right had never previously existed? Sir Henry Vane had accused Marten of 'impudence to affirme such a notorious Lye'. But Marten,

> standing up meekely replied, that there was a Text had much troubled his spirit for severall dayes and nights, of the man that was blind from his mothers womb whose Sight was restored, – at last – i.e. was restored to the sight which he should have had.

England always *should* have been free is the meaning here, so its 'FREEDOME' could indeed be 'RESTORED' exactly as its 'just and ancient Right' was something to which it could be returned. If Aubrey's anecdote is true, then it is an example not just of Marten's aptitude in citing the Bible (he combines three different texts) but another illustration of his brilliance 'in apt Instances' that Aubrey also praises.[9]

And then, to conclude this list of Marten's encounters with the House of Lords, although the process of the abolition of the Lords had been carried out in parallel with the 'Act for taking away Kingship', it had first been 'Resolved, &c.' in the Commons on 6 February 1649 that 'the House of Peers in Parliament is useless and dangerous, and ought to be abolished: And that an Act be brought in, to that Purpose'. Marten was appointed to the committee chosen to consider the Act and – in the words of a gossipy royalist commentator forty years later – 'Hereupon the Rump Vote the Lords Dangerous and Useless, yet *Henry Martin* said, they were Useless, but not Dangerous'.[10] Probably every member of the upper House would have heard about that little insult – just what a man about to plead for his life to them thirteen years later would want in his back story.

8

Lords

A number of earls and dukes – just thirteen on their first day – had celebrated their revived existence as the House of Lords on 25 April 1660 following the activities of General Monck, with the Commons agreeing to their reconstitution on 26 April. Since then the House had been reasserting some of its old power as one of the branches of government. In November 1661 it had finally been returned to its old size, composition, and function, with Lords Spiritual (Bishops) and Lords Temporal (nobility) back in their old roles, as the king had happily pointed out at the opening of parliament on 20 November. The Lords would again scrutinise Bills received from the House of Commons and work through three readings, exactly as the Commons did, so that the Bills could be returned – amended where their Lordships deemed necessary – to the Commons, either to become Acts of Parliament with the king's assent or for further discussion and emendation.

It had taken two months for the Commons to deliver its Bill 'for the Execution of certain Persons attainted of High Treason' to the Lords, but on Wednesday, 29 January 1662, the House of Lords received it and immediately gave it its formal first reading. Just four days later, on Saturday, 1 February, the Lords would proceed to the second reading, which would also count as its own committee stage. They intended to get it through as quickly as possible:

ORDERED, That the Consideration of this Bill is committed
to a Committee of the whole House; and, for the more speedy
Dispatch, the House was presently adjourned into a Committee, to debate it.

But that debate 'of the whole House' would lead to a further
delay – not stemming from compassion for prisoners locked up
for eighteen months but from the desire to execute even more
regicides. What the Lords believed they had found was that

> there are the Names of Six Persons left out, which are included
> in the Act of Oblivion, and have been since attainted of
> High Treason: Therefore the Opinion of the Committee is,
> That there be a Conference with the House of Commons, to
> acquaint them with this, and desire to know the Reasons that
> induced them to leave them out in this Bill.

And that was approved in the Lords.

The numbers and names were a real problem, as they had
been ever since the summer of 1660. To recapitulate: twenty-
nine regicides had been tried at the Old Bailey in October 1660
and all found guilty; ten had been executed. Of the nineteen surviving, four had since died (Owen Rowe, seen by the Commons
in November, had died in December). Of the fifteen left, two
(John Downes and George Fleetwood) had deliberately not been
included in the list forwarded by the Commons, although they
remained in the Tower. Another four had been dispatched to
other prisons.

The House of Lords had seven extra names it was now asking
about: not only Downes and Fleetwood but Edmund Harvey,
Hardress Waller, Robert Lilburne, Simon Mayne, and Thomas
Wogan. Mayne had died as long ago as April 1661, and Harvey,
Waller, Lilburne, and Wogan were not in the Tower; Downes

and Fleetwood could, however, be produced, even though – or perhaps because – the Commons had at the last minute decided not to include them.

Representatives of the Commons and Lords met together in the Painted Chamber on Monday, 3 February to agree a list of names, and it then required a 'long debate' in the House of Lords on Wednesday, 5 February before the Lords decided that it was not going to be outdone in painstaking legal procedures by the House of Commons. The deadline of 30 January had long gone, but the Lords would now have the attainted men brought in front of it before completing its second reading and sending the Bill to its third reading; a third reading that would commit the men to execution. Their Lordships wanted, doubtless, to hear what the men had to say, by way of grovelling apology – were there some more deserving than others? The prisoners would be brought from the Tower – or, to be exact, 'the Bodies' would be: they had been sentenced to death; they were technically and legally dead, as the lord chancellor would explain to one of the prisoners when he was brought up in front of the Lords as 'a Person dead in Law, and condemned, for that Treason of murdering the late King'. The regicides being brought to them would be, the Lords believed,

> the Bodies of *Owen Rowe, Augustine Garland, Henry Smith, Henry Martin, Robert Titchborne, James Temple, Thomas Wayt, William Heveningham, Isaac Pennington, Peter Temple, Gilbert Millington, Vincent Potter*, and *Thomas Wogan*, mentioned in a Bill depending now before the Lords in Parliament, sent up from the House of Commons; and also that the said Lieutenant of *The Tower* and his Deputies shall bring, in like Safety, to the said Bar, at the same Time, the Bodies of *Edmond Harvey*, Sir *Hardres Waller, Robert Lylborne, Symon Mayne, John Downes*, and *George Fleetwood*; and, after the

Pleasure of this House is signified concerning the said Persons, to return them in Safety into the said *Tower of London*.

This was still a confused and messy requirement. Rowe had just died, Pennington and Potter were both dead, and Wogan was not in the Tower: Mayne was dead and Harvey, Waller, and Lilburne had been dispatched to other prisons. But two days later, on Friday 7th, eleven men could be produced, even if the remaining four could not, and the third occasion on which the regicides were expected to plead for their lives could commence.

※

We know – without many details, unfortunately – the substance of what each man said at the bar of the Lords. Individuals tried what they thought would work best. Augustine Garland, for example – first up – tried a tactic which, as a member of the House of Commons, he would have seen more than once, when prisoners were brought to the bar of the House: in the Lords he 'kneeled at the Bar until he was bid to stand up'. To each prisoner it was explained that the Lords wanted to hear 'why the said Bill should not be passed for his Execution'. It was still high treason of which they had all been convicted; its punishment was still hanging, drawing, and quartering.

In some ways it must have been worse for the prisoners (still more threatening) than the events at the Old Bailey in October 1660, when the group of six with Marten in it, for example, had known that whatever happened they would not be executed until the requisite Act of Parliament had been passed. But in February 1662 no such postponement could be expected. This *was* the Act of Parliament under very active consideration. The Lords was not going to turn itself into a Court of Appeal that might overturn the Old Bailey's verdict (no one was asking it to do that, and it would not have done it). All the Lords had to do was accept the Bill from the House of Commons, proceed via readings and committee stage to its own third reading, and then return it to the Commons with perhaps an amendment or two: a matter of days. Their options were just three: (1) outright rejection of the whole Bill, (2) amendments required, or (3) Bill passed, meaning execution (death sudden) for all those named. Life imprisonment (death lingering) was not an option.

Of Marten's little original group of six at the Old Bailey only three were still left (Marten, Millington, and Titchborne); two were dead and Lilburne had been sent as a prisoner to the isolation of Drake's Island in Plymouth Sound. We do not know how he or (more likely his relatives) had managed to get him out of the murderous process in London into (in effect) life imprisonment in exile; it does not seem likely that he was ever brought back to face the House of Lords any more than the other prisoners not confined to the Tower appear to have been (in fact, he died on Drake's Island in 1665).

Gilbert Millington was a man in his late sixties, once a landed proprietor in Nottinghamshire (and deputy lieutenant of the county), also a barrister and MP (but not a soldier). He had been chosen as a commissioner in 1649 doubtless because of his legal qualifications; now all he could do was apologise as profoundly as he could and reiterate his dependence on the proclamation (something the House of Commons had not found sufficient to deny the regicides' execution):

> ... being demanded what he could say why the Act for Execution of him should not pass; he confessed his hearty Sorrow for his Sin; and desired the Mercy of the King's Proclamation, upon the Confidence of which he came and rendered himself.

This was really all Millington could say, although in those last ten

words there was a hint of the unfairness with which he believed
he had been treated. But his 'hearty Sorrow for his Sin' was just
the kind of tactic he would have been advised to try – and after
eighteen months locked up in the Tower it was very likely true
as well.

Various other tactics were employed. Henry Smith insisted
that he had been 'under Force' to do what he had done back in
1649 as a commissioner 'compelled by reason of Soldiers'; he
also referred not just to 'the King's Proclamation' but to 'His
Majesty's Gracious Proclamation'. Robert Titchborne 'made a
long speech' explaining how 'he had Thoughts within himself
how to contrive his Escape, out of this his Native Country,
beyond the Seas' but had chosen instead to rely on the 'mercy
and Security offered by his Majesty'; he had now come 'to
acknowledge his Sorrow for his great Crime'. John Downes also
'made a long Narrative', saying that he had been forced to sign
the king's death warrant but nevertheless expressed 'his hearty
sorrow for the same' (he had already published a broadside
explaining that he had attempted to bring the court trying the
king to change its mind and accept the king's offer to address
parliament but that he had been overruled: 'I acknowledge my
self to have highly offended and need pardon, and do humbly
and professedly lay hold on His sacred Majesties gratious
pardon; and humbly implore the high and honourable *Parliaments* Pardon also'[1]). Hard to imagine anyone bettering *that* as
a plea. William Heveningham even brought with him 'a Paper
of what he had further to say on his Behalf' and handed it over.
James Temple simply remarked that he 'had nothing to justify,
but did condemn himself, and abhorred the Fact' of the king's
death, while George Fleetwood went one better than Millington
when expressing 'his hearty Sorrow for his great Sin'. All but one
of the prisoners, according to the records of the House of Lords,
specifically referred to the proclamation.

There are two versions extant of what Marten is supposed to have said. One comes in the memoirs of Edmund Ludlow, and it is not known what Ludlow's source can have been (he was in Lausanne in February 1662). One possible but unlikely source would have been a transcript by someone who had been there; another, also unlikely, would have been a transcript Ludlow had managed to acquire of the records of the House of Lords. The most likely is Ludlow's own effusive memorial reconstruction of what he had been told:

> I now stand condemned by an Howse of Commons. My life lyes at your mercey, or rather before your justice. The Howse of Comons I alwayes adored, you I have opposed. But this is not the same Howse of Commons I served and honoured; nor that which invited us to render ourselves upon promise of security as to our lives, and which gave us in effect the fayth of the nation to that end. You are the same Lords whom, though I opposed in relation to the constitution (it being inconsistent, as I humbly supposed, with the good of the publique), yet not as to your persons, knowing that there are among you many of singular worth and honour. And therefore (though contrary to all faith and common honesty) we are delivered to the slaughter by those from whom, as we deserved, so we expected better dealing. Yet cannot we have such unworthy thoughts of this Howse, to suspect that, contrary to the faith given, they will concurr with that which is proposed to them for the putting of the bloody sentence passed upon us in execution, and thereby contract the blood of the innocent on their head, and render such a blemish in the escussion of their potesterity as can never be defaced —[2]

There is a good deal more effusive Ludlow in that than brief and idiomatic Marten. It would also have been uncharacteristic of

Marten to have warned the Lords against 'shedding the blood of the innocent', as well as naïve and unwise of him to have said anything about a blot on their noble escutcheons 'such ... as can never be defaced', if the House of Lords was to accept the way the Commons had delivered the regicides 'to the slaughter' (language reminiscent of Ludlow's energetically religious style).

The other version of what Marten said comes from the *Journal of the House of Lords* as transcribed and published in the late eighteenth century. Marten stands out for actually being humorous: it seems likely that the quotation in the *Journal* reproduces at least some of the actual words he spoke. The phrasing is as elegant as anything he ever wrote.

> That Honourable House of Commons, that he did heretofore so idolize, had given him up to Death; and now this Honourable House of Peers, which he had so much opposed, especially in their Power of Judicature, is now made the Sanctuary for to fly to for his Life. He submitted himself to His Majesty's Gracious Proclamation; which he took Hold of, and rendered himself, and hopes to receive Mercy by it; and now submits himself to His Majesty and this House for Mercy.

The remark about the Lords (in spite of his opposition to them) as his 'Sanctuary' may have made one or two smile, even though he apparently said nothing about his 'great Crime' or his 'great Sin', did not 'condemn himself', and expressed no 'hearty Sorrow'. He never had done so, in fact, which was something the solicitor general at the October 1660 trial had taken pains to point out – 'I am sorry to see so little repentance' (*EIA* 249) – while Bridgeman, in his final address to the jury, had commented about Marten, as unpleasantly as possible, that

> *Marten* hath done that which looks forward more then

backward, I could wish with all my heart, he had looked more backward; that is, to repentance of that which is past, then obedience to that which is to come ... (*EIA* 256)

But Marten was not going to say he was sorry. He still believed he had done the right thing in 1649. He was staying loyal to his beliefs while enunciating the things necessary to ensure that he might now be allowed to live – but he was not going to pretend he had stopped believing what he did.

※

What happened then to him and to the other ten is ... entirely mysterious. Following all their individual appearances,

> Hereupon the Lord Chancellor did let the Lieutenant of *The Tower* know, 'That the Lords had no more to say to the Prisoners now brought, at this Time; therefore he should carry them back again to *The Tower* in Safety.'

And that is what Robinson must have done. Nothing more, however, is recorded in the *Lords Journal* as having been said or done about the prisoners. There is no record of any of the four missing regicides being brought up in front of the bar; there is (naturally) no record of a committee stage in the House of Lords, that having been incorporated into the second reading the previous week: but, most remarkably of all, there is no record of the Lords proceeding to a third reading. The Bill, with or without amendments, is never recorded as having been returned to the House of Commons to be presented to the king as an Act of Parliament. The Commons remained in session until 19 May 1662 when they were prorogued until 11 February 1663. Not only is there no record of the Bill being returned to the Commons, there is no further recorded discussion on the subject in the surviving journals of either the Lords or the Commons. James Heath, compiling his chronicle of events, could only summarise about the prisoners: 'They were remanded back again to the Towers from whence they came, and no further proceeding had concerning them.'[3]

The apparent lack of a decision in the Lords could be explained in various ways. It is conceivable that the Bill disappeared into what was once termed 'the limbo of uncompleted legislation'[4] because the Lords – rather than set in motion a procedure that would do nothing but lead to the execution of at least eleven and perhaps fifteen people who had already spent eighteen months and more in gaol – simply abandoned it.

That, however, sounds far more humanitarian than the House of Lords usually was, especially as, in this case, it was dealing with a group of people who had collectively done their very best to injure aristocracy and the Church, to sequestrate land and property belonging to the Lords, and to fine them heavily for their political allegiance – all that apart from also being the king's killers. And the Bishops, too, might well have believed that in a case concerning the sacred majesty of the king there was a good deal that it was incumbent upon them now to demand. Back in the summer of 1660 the solicitor general had reported that their Lordships, considering the regicides,

> did not think it fit nor safe for this Kingdom that they should live: Here they cannot live; nor abroad with Safety; for Danger to a Kingdom is not always within Doors; Their Life may give them Opportunity of tampering to the Working of Mischief abroad. Then, for the Honour of the Kingdom; first, in point of Justice, Blood requires Blood; and he instanced in the *Gibeonites*, the shedding of their Blood could not be expiated but by the shedding of Blood.[5]

The blood lust of the House of Lords in August 1660 makes it appear all the stranger that only eighteen months later their Lordships should have passed up their chance to deal once and for all with the regicides.

One thing would have helped the regicides after April 1662. Three commissioners (John Okey, John Barkstead, and Miles Corbet), who had escaped to the Continent in 1660, would be tricked into capture in Delft in the Netherlands, and in March 1662 would be brought back to England. Imprisoned in the Tower, they would – after a brief hearing – be drawn, hanged, and quartered in April. The regicides surviving in the Tower were not like them, having given themselves up to the king's mercy, and from April 1662 onwards it might have been thought that they should not now suffer the same fate for what might be seen as a lesser crime (although there is no evidence of that argument having been offered).

This solution to the problem would acquire a great deal more force if it could be shown that although the regicides in the Netherlands were only brought back in March 1662 they had actually been arrested earlier, with their arrest being known about in government circles in England. But although Sir George Downing's plans to arrest the three had started in the autumn of 1661 everything was kept utterly secret until the arrest actually happened – which was not until 16 March 1662, a week before the three men were ingeniously, urgently, and after many bribes had been paid, shipped out of the Netherlands.[6] The idea does nothing to explain the lack of reported discussion of the regicides in either House of Parliament between mid-February and mid-March or why both the Lords and the Commons seem to have been prepared, in mid-parliamentary process, to abandon – without apparently protesting – a Bill on which they had both worked long and hard and with so many quarrels and disagreements.

The problem remains until, perhaps, one looks back at the

original terms of the decision to send the regicides to execution only after the passing of an Act of Parliament. These terms had been hammered out between the Lords and Commons on 25 August 1660:

> the Execution of the said Person and Persons, so attainted, shall be suspended, until his Majesty, by the Advice and Assent of the Lords and Commons, in Parliament, *shall order the Execution, by Act of Parliament* to be passed for that Purpose.

This means that if the Bill had passed through the Lords, as it had already passed through the Commons, then it would inevitably have gone to the king, who would then have had to agree to it as an Act of Parliament (as he did all Acts presented to him for his assent), so he would personally be ordering the execution of the fifteen men. One of the things with which Marten had tried to comfort Mary, when writing about the threat to execute him, was a report he had got wind of, in July or August 1660, of 'halfe a dozen Parliament men dining yesterday in Fish-street', who had been discussing the idea of the king simply 'pardoning' the regicides (*L* 46); he would later offer her the idea that the king might even be letting the process get to the point when the regicides in the Tower were about to be executed so as to reserve for himself 'the whole honour of pardoning' (*L* 66).

But if the king did not want to be seen pardoning the killers of his father there would have been one way for him to avoid a multiple death sentence. Someone very senior in the House of Lords – such as the lord chancellor, Edward Hyde, the official channel between the king and the Lords, or even the king's brother, the Duke of York – would have been able to make it known that the king wanted nothing more to happen (no extra regicides hauled up in front of the Lords, no third reading, no Bill returned to the Commons, nothing). The lord chancellor had been in the Lords on the 5, 6, 7, and 8 February; the Duke of York had heard the debate on the 5th, had heard the prisoners plead on the 7th, and was there again on the 8th. The king would in that way have been following his own 'Advice' and setting his own 'Example', as outlined by the lord chancellor on 8 May 1661 (see page 106). And that would have been that. Marten may have got it right at the very start when he had remarked at the Old Bailey of Charles II that 'I do owe my life to him, if I am acquitted for this' (*EIA* 250).

By holding back from their third reading, and so leaving the Bill stalled, the Lords thus saved the king the potential embarrassment and unpleasantness of ordering executions, but there was also no need for him to offer any kind of pardon.

The regicides – yesterday's men as they were – were thus simply abandoned to uncertainty and a fate which, by April 1662, might well have seemed to many people roughly right. If Charles II were prepared to live with the convicted and imprisoned regicides' continued existence, as he apparently was, that would have been enough, with the Commons also being quietly informed – unminuted – that the king saw the matter as being, for the moment, at an end, with the regicides confined to prison and remaining under sentence of death.

The effect of the whole grisly procedure, from November 1661 onwards – and this, too, may have been taken into account – would effectively have been to threaten the eleven prisoners in the Tower as much as possible at every stage, making them plead for their lives before the Commons, showing them they had not succeeded, giving them the example of three fellow commissioners being hauled on sledges to Tyburn in rehearsal for bloody execution, and themselves having to prepare for a final, all-or-nothing pleading for their lives to the Lords, making their pleas to the best of their abilities, and then never hearing anything more, thus leaving them to wake up every morning for the next few months wondering if they would find their execution planned for that day, or even, perhaps, being woken up in their prison by the arrival of the hurdles/sledges that would transport them to it. When, for example, in mid-April 1662 the three newly recovered regicides (Barkstead, Okey, and Corbet) were due for execution, other prisoners in the Tower would have heard the extraordinary noise heard by Barkstead – himself once Lieutenant of the Tower, now a prisoner sentenced to death – on the morning of his execution: 'the sledge[s], about eight o'clock, came into the Tower ... making a great noise upon the stones'.[7]

The sentence of death upon the regicide prisoners was never – as is sometimes assumed – commuted to imprisonment for life. They remained 'bodies', dead men, penniless, their possessions and estates taken from them; in prison, ripe for execution, unable to appeal against wrongful imprisonment, dying from age and disease, they were in some cases the 'living Monuments of their own Wretchedness', which one MP (moving *'for Banishment or Imprisonment'* as a solution to the regicide problem, back in August 1660) had described. All they could now do was wait for the sound of the sledges.

That ignominious but also terrifying fate was imposed upon fourteen of the fifteen men in question, the fifteenth – Thomas Wogan – only evading it by managing to escape from his prison in York Castle in 1664 and fleeing to the Continent. He was an example of exactly what was feared from the surviving regicides. His escape from York had been organised so that he could lead an insurrection in Gloucester in the late summer of 1663, and even when that failed to materialise and he had made his escape to the Netherlands, in 1666 he was reported to be again attempting to plot against the English government. It was clearly best to keep the regicides locked up, to be executed if ever it seemed right.

It is unlikely that anyone could ever have deliberately planned such a fate for them. The Commons could not have predicted at the end of January exactly how the House of Lords might react. The Lords might have passed the Bill through the committee stage and its third reading and sent it straight back to the Commons for it to be acted upon the following week and submitted to the king for his assent. And executions must inevitably have followed.

※

Renewed proceedings, which led to the execution of Sir Henry Vane on 14 July 1662, would, furthermore, show that the fate of regicides condemned to prison, even at a huge distance away, might at any moment be altered. Vane − not a commissioner but one of the most significant men in the various parliaments of the interregnum, once chairman of the Council of State and excluded from the Act of Indemnity − had been arrested in July 1660 and confined to the Tower of London until October 1661, when he had been sent to the Isles of Scilly to continue his prison sentence. In that way he was in a comparable situation to regicides like Hardress Waller, Henry Smith, James Temple, Millington, and Wayte, all of whom had ended up in prison on the island of Jersey.

But on 22 November 1661 it had been resolved in the Commons 'That the King's Majesty be desired to send for *John Lambert* and Sir *Henry Vane*, back again to the *Tower* of *London*, in order to their Trial', and on 19 February 1662 parliament again

Ordered: That his Majesty be again humbly moved to give Order for the present bringing back of Sir *Henry Vane* and *John Lambert*, in order to their speedy Tryal: And that Indictments be forthwith preferred against them: And that the Petition of Sir *Henry Vane*'s Tenants be presented to his

Majesty: And that his Majesty be desired to take the same into his Princely Consideration.

This shows that the Commons was insistent about Vane and Lambert, and it could easily have been equally insistent about any – or all – of the other fifteen regicides, just as it had apparently been in November 1660 when sending the Bill for their execution to the Lords. Charles had been happy to agree to Vane being brought back from his exile on the Scilly Isles in February when it had occurred simultaneously with the other regicides being left dangling (to use another seriously dead metaphor) in the hands of the House of Lords.

Lambert confessed his sorrow for everything that had been done and was – like the other regicides – again confined to prison (he ended up on Drake's Island). Vane defended himself brilliantly at his trial in July 1662, but his arguments (like those offered at the Old Bailey in October 1660) were ruled out by the fact that he had compassed and imagined the king's death and was therefore guilty. And apparently because of the particular desire of Charles II (who, as early as 1660, had spoken of Vane and others being 'of such dangerous principles that the safety of the nation cannot consist with their liberty'[8]) Vane would be executed in the Tower on 14 July 1662, although he had done a good deal less towards causing the death of Charles I than many others – which may have been one reason why his sentence of drawing, hanging, and quartering was commuted to execution; it was the king's prerogative to commute it, and Charles had no desire to have Vane butchered, only dead. Others (less dangerous than Vane from the point of view of the monarch) were for the moment left until some other reason, such as a republican rising, might have provoked calls for their execution. They were never reprieved; they remained on what we would today call death row.

※

It is quite unnecessary to think of Marten's survival as somehow special as nearly every commentator has done, while one scholar sounded actually shocked that he was not condemned: 'Inexplicably, Henry Marten alone among those tried for executing the King had received a suspended sentence.'[9] It has been assumed that Marten was not condemned in the House of Lords because 'Some of the lords ... must have recalled that Marten had often intervened to save the lives of royalists.'[10] There is, however, evidence of only a single intervention, a joke Marten had made in the House of Commons back in 1652 on behalf of the poet Sir William Davenant, who had asked him to do what he could.[11] Marten had then commented that sacrifices should be 'without spot or blemish', but 'now you are going to make an old rotten rascal a sacrifice' (Davenant was notorious for the ravages he had suffered from syphilis). And Davenant had survived.

Still further arguments suggest that Marten may not have been condemned

> because influential royalists were reluctant to create a martyr
> from someone of his personal notoriety. It may also have been
> because he was active in arguing for the lives of royalists when
> supporters of the high court of justice of the Commonwealth
> wanted retribution for war crimes that extended beyond solely
> the figure of Charles Stuart.[12]

Again, there is no evidence at all for the first of those speculations and precious little – only his help for Davenant – for the second. Bishop Burnet's version of events has also been quoted as if, somehow, it contained the truth:

One person escaped, as was reported, merely by his vices:

Henry Martin, who had been a most violent enemy to monarchy, but all that he moved for was upon Roman or Greek principles. He never entered into matters of religion, but on design to laugh both at them and at all morality; for he was both an impious and vicious man, and now in his imprisonment he delivered himself up unto vice and blasphemy. It was said that this helped him to so many friends, that upon that very account he was spared.[13]

But the bishop is, as so often, prejudiced and wrong. In his imprisonment Marten – except by occasionally getting to see Mary Ward – had had no chance at all of delivering himself up to vice, and even if he had been able to it would not have got him off. It would, too, be very hard to name those in the House of Lords who might be described as his 'many friends', and besides, were the other fourteen regicides all equally unprincipled?

Aubrey on the other hand reported a convincing-sounding story that Lord Falkland saved Marten's life by repeating the wry comment Marten had used to help save Davenant. When Marten was also facing the death penalty, according to Aubrey,

the Lord Falkland saved his life by Witt, saying – *Gentlemen!*
yee talke here of makeing a Sacrifice; it was old Lawe, all
Sacrifices were to be without spott, or blemish; and now you
are going to make an old Rotten Rascall a Sacrifice. This witt
tooke in the House and saved his Life.[14]

John Forster would agree with and reproduce the story ('Lord Falkland and other peers spoke very warmly in his behalf, and the sentence of death was remitted'[15]). But there is confusion here. In 1661–2, 'Lord Falkland' – in fact, Henry Cary, 4th Viscount Falkland – sat in the House of Commons not the House of Lords, and nothing said in the Commons in January had done anything to save Marten's life. On the contrary, the Commons had given the Bill its third reading and had forwarded it to the Lords.

It is, of course, possible either that Cary made the joke in the Commons at some point or that some other titled person made it in the House of Lords in February 1662 while they were discussing the regicides, but it seems quite wrong that 'This witt tooke in the House'. The crucial fact remains that all fifteen regicides were spared, not just Marten. Neither Marten's cleverness nor some Lord's warmth nor Titchborne's reported success 'in arguing for the lives of royalists' (in fact, for the life of a vintner and perhaps for Sir John Robinson) during the interregnum can be held responsible for the survival of all of them. But it is also significant that 'the sentence of death' was not remitted, not for Marten, not for anyone. As Jeremy Taylor had put it just eleven years earlier, all our 'quarrels and contentions' are ended by our 'passing to a final sentence' of death.[16]

※

We need to look for the explanation of Marten's survival during the years following his imprisonment in the Tower to some simple matters of fact. In the first place, although in his early sixties he was better able to survive the problems of a prison regime than others. His slanderers had written about him as raddled with the pox; in reality he had an extremely strong constitution – 'I have been on bare boord a thousand times in my life' (L 6) he once remarked to Mary Ward. Crucially, too, he remained, unlike others, able to get food himself and even supply Mary Ward with provisions at least some of the time he was in the Tower, and this because his extended family had helped him out after he had been rendered penniless. It turned out to have been highly intelligent of him to have had all those daughters, with a number of them marrying wealthy men. It looks as if family support was able to ensure his continued existence down to the end of his time in the Tower, and then right down to 1680.

Of those prisoners taken before the House of Lords in February 1662 – and the four not taken, because already elsewhere – all but one died in prison, four of them in the 1660s; while the fact that four men had already actually died in prison between 1660 and 1662, also suggests how testing the prison regime could be. John Downes is a case in point. Although apparently considered for release in February 1662 he remained 'in prison and in poverty' – and utterly miserable, too. 'In April 1663 he appealed to John Robinson, the lord mayor, begging to be "thrust into some hole where he might silently be slain"', 'alms and benevolence failing him' (he had already declared himself 'but a weak imprudent man').[17] The date of his death is unknown, although it was after November 1666 when he was listed as still in the Tower. But there is nothing like a good diet and warmth in winter – and if possible a cheerful disposition – to help a prisoner survive and to resist disease and infection. Marten tells Mary what a 'very great blessing' it is

> that you have all your healths, as I have mine, *I* thank God. Methinks, when *I* have that, and meet an enemy (of what kind soever) I am able to keep him at swords point; when I want that, he is got within me, and it requires a huge strength of heart to keep one's ground, when both sides are set upon at once ... (*L* 6)

A crucial year for them all seems to have been 1664, when warrants for transportation to Tangier were issued for at least one and perhaps two regicides (Garland and Fleetwood) and threatened for another (Hutchinson). Tangier, acquired in 1661 because of the forthcoming marriage of Charles II to Catarina de Bragança, was a death trap, with its English residents exposed to all kinds of new diseases in torrid temperatures. By 1664, too, another regicide had died in the Tower (Peter Temple in December 1663), but of the others, five ended up in Jersey (Millington, Smith, James Temple, Waller, Wayte), one in Windsor (Heveningham), Marten in Chepstow (having originally been sent to Berwick and then Windsor), one in Cornwall (Harvey), one (Lilburne) on Drake's Island, one in Dover (Titchborne until 1674), while only one seems never to have left the Tower of London (Downes, probably regarded as neither dangerous nor a potential focus for political dissent).

The different places where the men were finally imprisoned may have had something to do with their record (Garland perhaps still affected by the story told at the trial in 1660 that he had spat in the king's face – something he strenuously denied, but which may have remained an influence) but would primarily have been because of continuing anxiety, originally in the winter of 1661–2 but on many occasions subsequently, about plots to overturn or at least destabilise the regime and to re-establish a republic. This was linked with fear of regicides like Wogan either initiating or being directly involved in such plots. It seemed sensible, therefore, to dispatch them as far from London (and the possibility of republican rebellion in favour of the 'good old cause') as possible. Having been threatened with Tangier early in 1664 Hutchinson was at first ordered to be dispatched to the Isle of Man but was finally sent to Sandown Castle, near Deal, almost as far east in Kent as it is possible to go, right at the edge of the sea. The place was ruinous and the damp conditions had wretched consequences for his health; he would die there in 1664. But he had been one of those accused of recently plotting; he was supposed to have shouted out of his window at the Tower, when two other prisoners were being moved, that they must 'take courage they should yet have a day for it'.[18]

Another factor influencing where prisoners ended up and the conditions of their lives in prison would have been money. Lodgings in the Tower were notoriously expensive: Sir John Robinson demanded £50 from Hutchinson for the first six months he had been in prison there, and people may have been moved (or even transported) according to their family's unwillingness to pay for them (or to bribe middle men). Marten's financial affairs were in tatters long before he turned himself in in June 1660; during the 1660s indeed, there were various legal actions initiated by people who had acquired land from him (land already loaded with debts and mortgages). He even had trouble with his own brother-in-law, Lord Lovelace, who took legal action against him for the repayment of moneys owed, as well as from John Loder, to whom he had sold land in the late 1650s.

But no anecdotes of men reprieved because they had helped royalists in the interregnum, or because their lives had been pleaded for (in return for money) by those at court, or because of appeals to the king, or because they had said witty or memorable things seem to have had any effect upon their ultimate fate, even though all these things may have occurred.

The eleven regicides who went through the gamut of the whole legal process of Old Bailey, Commons, and Lords were, at any rate, abandoned to die in prison, along with the others already scattered around Britain, most of them at a great distance from London, friends, and family (which would not only have had the effect of getting them out of the way of republican plotters but also of cutting them off from family subsidy). Of all the regicides who died in prison only two would survive as long as 1680.

And the one who lived to the greatest age – eight years older than the other, Robert Titchborne, when he died – was Henry Marten, the most extraordinarily tough and resilient character.

9

Ghostless in Chepstow

Some endings arrive not with a bang but not with a whimper either: Marten was not the whimpering sort. The extended trials for the regicides were over, and – after all – nothing had happened. For those who had survived the Old Bailey there had been no more terrible endings, with prayer, rage, blood, guts, no relieving nor awful culminations. Instead, nearly all of the surviving regicides, including Marten, effectively vanished, being sent as prisoners to gaols as far from London as possible. A still longer period of trial for them all was only just beginning but one which was in effect a death sentence, being one they would never outlive.

On 25 July 1662 Sir John Robinson was ordered to have Marten transferred to the ship *Anne* so that he could be transported from the Tower up to Berwick, on the Scottish border,[1] a voyage around the east coast (sending prisoners by sea rather than by land being more secure). Marten may have been taken to the Castle near the harbour at Berwick; he may have been transferred immediately to the extreme remoteness of the Holy Island Castle, five or six miles further south. It was apparently from here that less than three years later, on 19 May 1665, he was transported back south to Windsor Castle. This seems odd, given the distances to which most of the other regicides had been transported. It was almost certainly because his brother-in-law John, 2nd Lord Lovelace, Lord Lieutenant of Berkshire

– the county in which Windsor lay – had successfully petitioned for him to be returned somewhere nearer the Lovelace home at Hurley, just ten miles from Windsor.

Two things seem to have contributed to his removal from Windsor three years later in 1668. One was the fact that the constable in charge at Windsor, John Lord Viscount Mordaunt, had lost his job because of various reported irregularities – the crucial one being that he had allowed '*Henry Martin*, a Traitor, one of the late Regicides, then a Prisoner there ... to go abroad out of the said Castle, without a Keeper'. Lord Mordaunt had protested to the House of Commons that this was completely untrue:

> as for *Henry Marten's* Liberty, his Lordship saith, it was not done with his Privity or Consent; but saith, he hath since enquired thereinto, and finds the Fact to be, that the Lord *Lovelace*, being Lord Lieutenant of the County, coming to *Windsor*, sent to the Officer, to desire Leave for *Henry Marten* (his Brother-in-law) to dine with him, who accordingly gave him Leave, and sent the Marshal with him, who brought him back again.[2]

Lovelace, for all his financial unhappiness with his old brother-in-law, was still on dining terms with him. But Mordaunt lost his job, which can't have helped Marten's chances at Windsor. The other ground for his being 'removed from thence' was because (Aubrey believed) Charles II was annoyed at the sight of him: 'he was an eie-sore to his Majestie'.[3] Perhaps he had been walking the walls at Windsor (we know the pleasure he took in walking 'the leads' at the Tower). Whatever the truth of it, in December 1668 Marten was ordered to the far distant outpost of Chepstow on the Welsh border.

Chepstow Castle had at various times been occupied by the

king's forces during the Civil War until in May 1648 it had been severely damaged when four Parliamentarian guns on a nearby hill 'put in battery against it'. Its southern curtain wall had been breached, and the castle had fallen. It was then garrisoned by a company of soldiers, the medieval curtain wall being rebuilt and substantially thickened, with earth packed between two stone walls like the filling of a sandwich to give it a chance of surviving another bombardment. Its parapet was also 'loopholed for musketry', in a further attempt to adapt a medieval structure to modern weaponry and to render it secure as castle and prison. The new castle garrison – of around seventy men – 'was regarded as vital to the maintenance of law and order in the district'; in 1661 it was rumoured that local anti-royalists, often Fifth Monarchists – commonly known as 'the fanatick party'[4] – were a threat. The castle continued to be manned and garrisoned until 1690, after which it was abandoned as there seemed no likelihood of rebellion in the district.[5]

It was in the period between around 1653 and 1690 that it was also used as a prison for political and military prisoners; the royalist cleric and writer Jeremy Taylor was imprisoned here between May and October 1655. We know rather little about Marten's time in Chepstow, but there is one surviving feature of the castle that can remind us directly of him. The original castle gates – their wood dating from the 1190s – still survive, the oldest castle gates in Europe; the beautiful mortise-and-tenon latticework of the inside of the gates being exactly what Henry Marten would have confronted every day during his twelve years there.

The castle commemorates him in the 'splendid tower at the south-east angle of the castle, generally known today as Marten's Tower', finished around 1300 and still roofed at the end of the eighteenth century. The first record of a visit to it appears to be in a 1789 travel book by the Reverend Stebbing Shaw, who noted that

Illustration 15: Oak gates of Chepstow Castle (by 1190)

In one of the towers we saw the room where Harry Martin, one of the twelve judges, who sat to condemn Charles I. was afterwards confined for 27 years, and then died there. From the leads above, we had an extensive and fine view. In another place we saw the traces of a large chapel.[6]

Illustration 16: 'Marten's Tower', Chepstow Castle:
engraving by Richard Colt Hoare, 1798

Illustration 16 shows pretty well what Stebbing Shaw must
have seen, along with extra buildings then standing in the lower
bailey. Having in effect been left to decay since the end of the
seventeenth century, however, the tower's roof fell in some time
soon after, and the floors went, too; the castle was uninhabited
from the late nineteenth century onwards.

It is hard today to imagine Marten's Tower as it may have
been in his time with four floors: a basement, a hall for the lord

of the castle on the second floor, his main chamber on the third, and smaller rooms at the top under the roof. How much of this accommodation Marten occupied (and what its condition then was) is impossible to tell; the usual practice seems to have been to charge a prisoner rent on the rooms he inhabited, in which case it seems likely that the older Marten grew – and the poorer – the less accommodation he would have been able to afford: he may have ended up in one of the rooms at the top. The fact that the main chamber has recently been refloored actually makes it harder to understand the original layout of the tower.

But Marten's original room would probably have had window seats under the original lancet windows on the outer wall, on the right in Illustration 17, the same enormous fireplace and (not here visible) a large sixteenth-century window looking into the castle's lower bailey. It would also have been possible for Marten to gain access to the parapets running west along the (then) newly rebuilt and loopholed curtain wall directly from his room, one opening being to the left of the fireplace. This would have afforded him even better fresh air than 'the leads' in the Tower of London or the walls at Windsor had done as well as offering marvellous views over Chepstow and the country beyond, and it seems likely that he would have been able to go out on 'the leads' at the very top of his tower, as Stebbing Shaw did in 1788, up the circular staircase on the left in Illustration 17.

※

There are five principal sources of information about Marten's time – probably twelve years – in Chepstow. The first is Aubrey (born 1626) with his observation that 'During his Imprisonment his wife relieved him, out of her joincture. but she dyed'.[7] A jointure is property held, originally, for the joint use of husband and wife for life but also as a provision for the latter in the event of

Illustration 17: 'Marten's Tower', main chamber with modern floor

her widowhood; in Marten's case (according to the analysis of his financial position carried out on his condemnation to death), £400 a year had been allocated 'for his wife's jointure, made before marriage, above 20 years since'. But Margaret Marten was now a widow, her husband being 'dead in law', and it appears that she could have continued in possession of property and income. If indeed she contributed to Marten's support in Chepstow – Aubrey's 'relieved' implies assistance but no more – that suggests that his other possibilities of support had grown inadequate, the woman with whom he had not lived for thirty years in the end helping to maintain him.[8] When *she* died (in January 1680) the money from her jointure would have stopped, too.

One of the useful things in the second source of information about Marten in Chepstow – Anthony Wood's account – is a reference to 'his Daughter, who usually attended him' in Chepstow. Wood may be right about this. In London the daughter who seems to have engaged in most care for Marten in the Tower was Jane (Jinny, Jennie), his third daughter by Margaret, born in 1638. She it was who back in 1657 had called herself 'your most obedient child till death',[9] and since – so far as we know – she never married, she may have come to Chepstow, assisted financially by her mother, hence Aubrey's belief that Margaret Marten's jointure helped support Marten.

Wood goes on, in his usual knowing style, to insist that in Chepstow Marten 'lived very poor and in a shabbed condition in his confinement, and would be glad to take a pot of ale from any one that would give it to him'. That is not actually contradictory to the idea of a daughter coming to take care of him: by the 1670s, the Marten family may well not have been able any longer to go on paying for servants for him, so family (in the person of Jane) would have had to step in. Wood's sources for his knowledge of Marten in Chepstow are unknown; born in 1632 he is extremely unlikely to have known Marten personally (he did not go to London until 1667) but writes about him as if he had, describing how Marten was

> a man of good natural parts, was a boon familiar, witty, and quick with repartees, was exceeding happy in apt instances, pertinent and very biting; so that his company being esteemed incomparable by many, would have been acceptable to the greatest persons, only he would be drunk too soon, and so put an end to all the mirth for the present.[10]

For that, however, he is almost entirely dependent on Aubrey, whose notes record how Marten was 'of an incomparable witt for Reparte's', that 'He was exceeding happy in apt Instances', and also characterise Marten's speech as 'pertinent'.[11]

What, though, is helpful in Wood's writing is his stress on Marten's 'confinement' in Chepstow. Too many accounts from the late eighteenth and early nineteenth centuries are – because of the dearth of other information – concerned with Marten's visits outside the castle at Chepstow (for example, from 1801, 'In the course of years, political rigor against him began to wear away; and he was permitted ... to walk about Chepstow'[12]). Wood, however, remained a long way from Chepstow, and it was not until December 1680 that he even heard of Marten's death, inscribing in his diary:

> In the beginning of this month I was told that Harry Marten died last summer, suddenly, with meat in his mouth, at Chepstow in Monmouthshire.[13]

It has been assumed that Marten died at 'supper' in September 1680 and that may be true (although why 'supper' rather than 'dinner' is unclear). But Wood is referencing the Bible, most notably Psalm 78.30, in which the wrath of God falls on people 'while the meat was yet in their mouths'. Wood means unexpectedly; what he wrote does not support references to Marten choking to death.

The third – and major – source of information about Marten in Chepstow is a book, including a long description of town and castle, assembled and partly written by Charles Heath, drawing on local anecdotes and first published in 1793 but republished with a good deal more material at various times in the early nineteenth century. By 1801, for example, Heath's description of Marten's main chamber had turned into this:

> This room measures fifteen paces long, by twelve paces wide, and very lofty. On one side, in the centre, is a fire-place two yards wide: and the windows, which are spacious, and light both ends of the apartment, give it an air of cheerfulness unknown to such places ... though the rafters and floor, *from damp and lapse* of time, are in a very decayed state ...[14]

Heath also adds something to the likelihood that Marten's family took over the care of him towards the end of his life:

> For twenty years of his confinement, Marten was denied the attendance of his family, during which time, an ancestor of Mrs. Williams (who lives in the Castle), and another woman were the persons who waited on him. Afterwards, his *two daughters* were admitted, who continued with him during the remainder of his life.[15]

That turns the history of Marten's descent into poverty (so that his children were obliged to care for him) into a touching account of how he reacquired his family late in life: 'he was permitted ... to have the constant residence of his family, in order to attend upon him, allowed him in the Castle'.[16]

Heath's source was Mrs Williams, who had been wife to the keeper of Chepstow Castle, a woman in her eighties (she died in 1798), one of whose ancestors had been alive in Marten's time. Marten, however, remained the castle's most famous prisoner, and information may well have been passed down to succeeding generations. Mrs Williams explained that two sisters, Catherine and Margaret Vick, whom she claimed to know very well, were 'the women who waited and attended on Harry Marten, during his confinement'.[17] The dates add up: if the sisters had been in their teens or early twenties when they worked for Marten in the early 1670s, before his daughter came, they could have been born in the 1650s and lived on until 1730 or thereabouts, so Mrs Williams (born around 1708) could have known them when she was a young woman.

The idea that Marten managed some kind of a social life outside the prison with the neighbouring gentry is especially developed in the longest anecdote that Heath provides. He explains how

Indulgence at last extended itself so far, as to permit him to visit any family in the neighbourhood, – *his host being responsible for his safe return to the Castle at the hour limitted.*[18]

By 1793 a portrait in the possession of the Lewis family, of the parish and hamlet of St Pierre, had been identified as of Marten.[19] The family's house was about three miles south-west of Chepstow; for Marten, in his seventies, to get there and back would possibly have required some kind of transport (they may have sent him a horse for his visits).

But some information, derived from the Vick sisters, survives of his visiting the Lewises:

Among other families who paid Mr. Marten attention, were the ancestors of the present worthy possessor of Saint Pierre, near Chepstow. A large company were assembled round the festive dinner board, to which Marten had been invited; – soon after the cloth was removed, and *the bottle put in gay circulation*, Mr Lewis, in a cheerful moment, jocularly said to Marten, 'Harry, suppose the times were to come again in which you passed your life, what part would you act in *them?*' – '*The part I have done,*' was his *immediate reply*. 'Then Sir, says Mr. Lewis, I never desire to see you at my table again,' – nor was he ever after invited.[20]

That sounds credible, expressing as it does Marten's straightforwardness (Aubrey summed him up as 'honest'[21]), his preparedness to be awkward, and his continuing lack of repentance. An engraving from 1799 (Illustration 18) shows the medieval gatehouse, which originally formed a considerable part of the St Pierre manor house; the entrance is just as Marten would have seen it, with various roof extensions (now removed) and further parts of the house behind. The building on the right, with the

Illustration 18: St Pierre gatehouse and church:
engraving by Richard Colt Hoare, 1798

porch, is the little church. The view has not changed much since
the 1670s.

Heath also provides an anecdote for which he offers the testimony of 'a friend':

> Of his Person. – a friend of mine, on the authority of the
> late *Mr. Harry Morgan, Attorney, at Usk,*[22] – whose father
> had been in Marten's company, and by whom he had been
> informed of it, – told me that Mr. Morgan described him in
> general terms, 'as a smart, active little man, and the merriest
> companion he ever was in company with in his life.'

This anecdote can also be seen as having some potential relationship with historical fact. The 'Harry Morgan' recorded by
Heath as having been in Marten's company would have been

(in a Caerleon family in which every generation contained a lawyer named Henry Morgan) the one born in 1644, and so aged between twenty-three and thirty-six during Marten's time in Chepstow. *His* son – a Sheriff in Monmouthshire in 1722 – was probably born too late to have known Marten but might not have died until the 1740s. The 'friend' of Heath would have got his information from the second Henry Morgan (in which case the friend was probably aged seventy or so when he passed on the information to Heath, presumably in the 1790s, but it would indeed have been Morgan's father who had been the original source). Morgan's anecdote corresponds to what Aubrey had once written about Marten: 'Sir Edward Baynton [*sic*] was wont to say that his company was incomparable but that he would be drunke too soon.'[23] Morgan's account (although without Bayntun's qualification) suggests that Marten had retained his capacity for charm and liveliness into his seventies; and 'a smart ... little man' – Aubrey had noted that 'his stature was but midling' – had not yet been reduced to the 'shabbed condition' Wood stresses, although 'a pot of ale' may still have been attractive (we might think of the quantities of beer and wine issuing from the Tower of London while Marten was there).[24]

The fourth source for information about Marten in Chepstow is Coxe's *Historical Tour in Monmouthshire* of 1801, which draws on Heath but also includes the results of Coxe's own researches. These are mostly to Marten's disadvantage, but are also responsible for starting a number of myths about Marten that continue to our own time: for example, that 'His wife was permitted to reside with him'. Of that there is no evidence and it seems most unlikely (we know that she died in Longworth in Berkshire), while Mary Ward could never have been referred to in such terms. Coxe also declares that Marten 'had the full enjoyment of his property' (which we know not to have been the case), 'and was allowed to receive visits, and to frequent, in company with a guard, the houses of the neighbouring gentry, particularly that of St. Pierre, where his portrait is still preserved' (Coxe, ii. 389). That information is drawn from Heath. Coxe goes on to argue that 'His situation could not be distressed, as Mrs. Williams [the same woman who was Heath's informant] recollected two of his maid servants [presumably the Vick sisters], who always mentioned him as a kind master, and were able to save money in his service' (Coxe, ii. 389). Marten was generous when he could be, but it seems rather unlikely that he could have been any more than kind to his servants in Chepstow.

※

The final source of information about Marten in Chepstow is the epitaph he wrote and which appeared on his tombstone in St Mary's Church after his burial there on 9 September 1680; it is the only piece of his writing that we can be sure comes down from his years in Chepstow.

Wood was the first to cite the epitaph 'by way of Acrostick on himself' which he made 'Some time before he died'.[25] Marten's acrostic poem actually exists in multiple versions; and this is especially problematic as most of the original memorial slab in the chancel of the church no longer exists. Marten's burial in the church was, by order of the Vicar of Chepstow (1701–40), Thomas Chest, removed from the chancel to the nave. The catastrophic collapse of the eastern tower of the church in the first decade of the eighteenth century, which destroyed the existing chancel and transepts, probably led to the rearrangement. What may well have been the original slab had been severely damaged by 1800, as is shown in the version of it engraved by Thomas Jennings for Coxe's second volume (Illustration 19); it looks as if it had been broken in half and that one side had also been badly

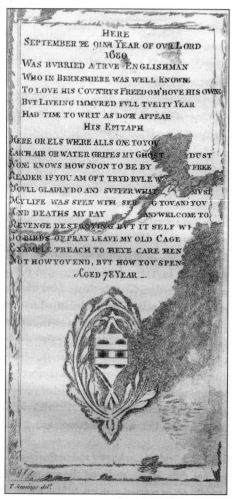

HERE
SEPTEMBER ᵗᴱ 9Iᴺᴴ YEAR OF OVᴿ Lᴏʀᴅ
1680
Was Bᴠʀʀɪᴇᴅ ᴀ Tʀᴠᴇ ᴇɴɢʟɪsʜᴍᴀɴ
Wʜᴏ ɪɴ Bᴇʀᴋsʜɪᴇʀᴇ ᴡᴀs ᴡᴇʟʟ Kɴᴏᴡɴᴇ
Tᴏ ʟᴏᴠᴇ ʜɪs Cᴏᴠɴᴛʀʏs Fʀᴇᴇᴅᴏᴍ ʙᴏᴠᴇ ʜɪs ᴏᴡɴᴇ
Bᴠᴛ Lɪᴠᴇɪɴɢ ɪᴍᴍᴠʀᴇᴅ Fᴠʟʟ ᴛᴠᴇɪᴛʏ Yᴇᴀʀ
Hᴀᴅ ᴛɪᴍᴇ ᴛᴏ ᴡʀɪᴛ ᴀs ᴅᴏᴛʜ ᴀᴘᴘᴇᴀʀ
Hɪs Eᴘɪᴛᴀᴘʜ

Hᴇʀᴇ ᴏʀ ᴇʟs ᴡʜᴇʀᴇ ᴀʟʟs ᴏɴᴇ ᴛᴏ ʏᴏᴠ
Eᴀʀ ᴛʜ ᴀɪʀ ᴏʀ ᴡᴀᴛᴇʀ ɢʀɪᴘᴇs ᴍʏ Gʜᴏsᴛ   ᴅᴠsᴛ
Nᴏɴᴇ ᴋɴᴏᴡs ʜᴏᴡ sᴏᴏɴ ᴛᴏ ʙᴇ ʙʏ   ᴛ Fʀᴇᴇ
Rᴇᴀᴅᴇʀ ɪғ ʏᴏᴜ ᴀᴍ ᴏғᴛ ᴛʀʏᴅ ʀᴠʟᴇ ᴡ
Yᴏᴠʟʟ ɢʟᴀᴅʟʏ ᴅᴏ ᴀɴᴅ sᴠғғᴇʀ ᴡʜᴀᴛ   ᴀᴠsᴛ
Mʏ ʟɪғᴇ ᴡᴀs sᴘᴇɴ ᴡɪᴛʜ sᴇʀ   ɢ ʏᴏᴠ ᴀɴᴅ ʏᴏᴠ
Aɴᴅ ᴅᴇᴀᴛʜs ᴍʏ ᴘᴀʏ   ᴀɴᴅ ᴡᴇʟᴄᴏᴍᴇ ᴛᴏ
Rᴇᴠᴇɴɢᴇ ᴅᴇsᴛʀᴏʏɪɴɢ ʙᴠᴛ ɪᴛ sᴇʟғ ᴡʜ
Sᴏ ʙɪʀᴅs ᴏғ ᴘʀᴀʏ ʟᴇᴀᴠᴇ ᴍʏ ᴏʟᴅ Cᴀɢᴇ
Exᴀᴍᴘʟᴇ ᴘʀᴇᴀᴄʜ ᴛᴏ ᴛʜᴇʏᴇ ᴄᴀʀᴇ ʜᴇɴ
Nᴏᴛ ʜᴏᴡ ʏᴏᴠ ᴇɴᴅ, ʙᴠᴛ ʜᴏᴡ ʏᴏᴠ sᴘᴇɴ
Aɢᴇᴅ 78 Yᴇᴀʀ ⹀

T Jennings del.

Illustration 19: Henry Marten's epitaph slab:
engraving by Thomas Jennings, *c*. 1800

damaged in the tower collapse. Either that tombstone, with the
pieces brought together, or a recut version of it, was relaid where
in 1795 James Baker remembered seeing it, 'flat on the ground
in the narrow passage leading from the middle into the north
aisle, and exactly opposite to the reading desk'. But by 1795 the

lettering on that slab had already been 'obliterated by people constantly walking over it'.[26]

Following the further rebuilding and reordering of the church in the nineteenth century (including the total removal of the north aisle in the 1840s), in 1895 the memorial was moved to yet another place, even further from the east end near the west door in the nave, with a recut inscription and an explanation: 'This stone which formerly marked the grave of Henry Marten was recut during the restoration of the church.' The ends of the lines on that recut epitaph are also now hard to read.

Fortunately, a fragment of the original stone now in Chepstow Museum, together with the engraving of the damaged slab and two printed sources, can help us reconstruct the earliest form of the epitaph. A version of the first stanza ('Harry Marten's Epitaph by Himself') was printed in *Examen Poeticum* in 1693, only twelve years or so after the stone can have been laid and before it was damaged or moved.[27] The earliest full printed version apparently dates from *Sepulchrorum Inscriptiones* of 1727 and shows some differences, not just in the inclusion of the extra six lines. The acrostic text below is based on that of the original stone, so far as it can be recovered (we have partly to trust to the accuracy of Coxe's engraving), emended – but only where entirely necessary – from the 1693 and 1727 texts:

Here or elsewhere alls one to you, to me
Earth air or water grips my ghostless dust
None knows how soon to be by fire set free
Reader if you an oft tried rule will trust
Youll gladly do and suffer what you must
My life was spent with serving you and you
And deaths my pay it seems and welcome too
Revenge destroying but itself while I
To birds of pray leave my old cage and fly

Example preach to th eye care then mine says
Not how you end, but how you spend your days
Aged 78 year

In 1801 Heath printed a version of the epitaph taken (in theory)
from his own examination of the memorial stone, which for the
most part corresponds with that version, but his text shows
how startling he found the word 'ghostless' in line 2: he substi-
tuted 'ghostly', the word he doubtless believed more decent and
proper. He was also extremely rude about the epitaph, calling
the lines 'wretched doggerels' that 'It is hardly possible to admit
that such a mind as Mr. Marten's would have penned.'[28]

For a man such as Marten, who was not a poet, it is all the
same a nice piece of work, as is confirmed by its partial arrival in
print less than thirteen years after it had appeared on his memorial slab. Can't do better than that now, we can imagine him
saying.

For even the first five lines reveal it as rather an odd piece
of work for a church memorial. Where exactly is the deceased
Henry Marten? His answer is 'Here or elsewhere', thus running
directly contrary to the traditional gravestone formula 'Here lies
...' (although weirdly foreshadowing the later perambulations
of grave, remains, and epitaph). Anyway, does it matter exactly
where? If it's 'all one' to the casual onlooker, it's certainly unim-
portant to Henry Marten. He is just dust.

But that dust of his which somewhere remains is also 'ghostless', in that most remarkable word. He has no soul, he is
emphatic in saying – until one day, when he will finally be set
free by 'brave fire': that is, his ghostless dust will finally not just
be fierily consumed but *excellently* consumed, and he (a prisoner
since 1660) will be free at last, disembodied at last, completely
gone at last. Those who took revenge on him, 'birds of pray' as
they are on the stone epitaph – revengeful in searching out prey

but also pious – go on being confined (by life, by revenge, by piety) just as he was once confined (by prison). But he will finally be free as the air, released to 'leave my old cage' (prison, grave, church, and all) 'and fly'.

The last line, too, 'seems to be a pointed rejoinder to the cult of the martyred Charles I'. For Marten,

> however beautiful Charles's death on the scaffold might have been, what counted was the wrongs he had done during his lifetime. Conversely, what counted in his own life was not the uncertain purchase he might or might not make on the nation's memory, but whatever practical good he had managed to do.

And his epitaph gives 'not even a perfunctory nod in the direction of conventional religion'.[29]

There were reasons enough there, even if Marten had not been a regicide and there had been no tower collapse, for Thomas Chest to have wanted the memorial slab – and perhaps the remains – moved out of the chancel and placed on (and under) the floor on the north side of the nave on their way, a century later, down to the west door. But in doing that, Chest assisted in the addition of yet another layer of fantasy to the first line of the poem. Where exactly *is* Marten now? Still buried in the chancel? Twice moved, along with epitaph and stone? What about the relaying of the slab in two new places? Was Marten completely moved along with it? As much as possible moved? Left where he was, just the 'stone which formerly marked the grave' moved? 'Here or elsewhere', he continues to defeat enquiry.

Wood remarks, in his characteristically irritating way, that there was 'Another Epitaph … made by his daughter who usually attended him' but that ('for brevity sake') he has to omit it.[30] It seems probable that he is referring to the four rhyming lines preceding the acrostic epitaph on the tombstone. It is hard to tell exactly who may have written what, but those lines were composed by someone who remembered Marten's origins in Berkshire. A daughter like Jane might well have done that and would also have known what he would have wanted said about his life: the lines on the inscribed stone version seem likely to be closest to the text as first written.

> Here
> September the 9 in the Year of our Lord
> 1680.
> Was burried a true Englishman
> Who in Berkshire was well knowne
> To love his countrys freedom'bove his owne
> But *liveing immured full twenty year*
> Had time to writ as doth appear
> His Epitaph [31]

It is fitting that those lines, too, should be exercised by the idea of freedom, not just Marten's own freedom taken away but the freedom demanded by a 'man of the present age' who, in so many ways, seems attuned to our own age (he even opposed legislation enabling the conscription of men for the Parliamentarian armed forces: it was 'against the liberty of the subject'.[32]) He never stopped believing that the English 'ought to be absolutely free from ... *Arbitrary Power*', and he had run every risk of a dreadful fate in his constant refusal to apologise either for the English republic or for the execution of Charles I.

He had indeed, in a letter probably of August 1660 – 'calling a Court at home' – tried himself 'at the bar of my own conscience', impartially assuming the roles not only of defendant but of witnesses and prosecution, and – demonstrating his cheerful acquaintance with Shakespeare's *A Midsummer Night's Dream* –

to the best of my understanding having acted *Pyramus* and *Thisbe*, the Lion and the Moon-shine ... *I* stood clearly acquitted upon the whole matter ... (*L* 1–2)

But although 'acquitted', Marten had regrets, not just those prudently expressed at the Old Bailey – 'My Lord, if it were possible for that Blood to be in the Body again, and every drop that was shed in the late Wars, I could wish it with all my heart' (*EIA* 249) – but the kind of regret a politician feels who has failed in his dearest ambition, as Marten confessed in the same letter:

> Could *I* have foreseen how dearly publick freedome must be bought, and how hardly it can be kept, *I* would have used onely my passive valour against all the late Kings oppressions, rather then voted, as *I* did, any War at all ... (*L* 3)

This is striking for a man who had in May 1647 been chairman of the 'committee for consideration of the liberties of the commons of England'.[33] But – given that there had been the Civil War, for which he had voted – he now saw the act in which one phase of the war culminated, the execution of the king, as simply its inevitable consequence: 'you must understand that this act, whether its name be Treason and Murther, or Reason and Justice, its Parent was a Civil War' (*L* 3).

But his own main goal, however unfortunately pursued, had always been 'publick freedome'; freedom from what in his levelling days back in 1647 he had provokingly termed the 'corrupt interests' of 'the Nobility, Gentry and Clergy', interests lying 'directly opposite to the interests of the people'. In 1648 he had actually started to compose a 'manifesto' directed 'against King, Lords, and Commons, as confederate to the enslaving of the people' and – if a popular newsbook is to be trusted – had gone so far as to equip some of his cavalry with banners displaying the characteristic motto 'For the People's Freedom against all tyrants whatsoever'.[34] But it was freedom awarded to and represented by the House of Commons that he meant, except perhaps during the time he was closest to the Levellers. By 1653, in his denunciatory farewell to Cromwell, he had been sure that 'the quiet, freedom, and happiness of England were "not to be expected but from a popular election"'. It was Marten's concern for 'publick freedome' during a career that, up to 1653, had been 'spent with serving you and you' – serving for as long as he had been allowed to pursue his political career – which arguably made him what Aubrey thought him, 'a great and faithfull lover of his Countrey'. Aubrey was echoing the encomium on Marten in the Parliamentarian newsbook *Mercurius Britanicus* in 1648, which had specified 'the noble love he bore his country'. In 1648, too, Marten had confessed to the kind of 'double engagement' to which he had found himself committed: 'one of my own making, the other made when I was born'.[35] He had been born into privilege and freedom and now believed in doing what he could to free others; of his 'own making' he had decided to engage in politics, before – at the age of fifty-one – being shunted out of all possibility of influence.

What happened to Mary Ward and the children? We have no idea. The relationship had probably effectively ended some time before the summer of 1662, simply because Mary Ward was in such financial straits that she had been forced to take a 'new Dear' or because she had had to move away and could neither visit Marten any more nor afford to send messengers with letters. It is impossible to tell when such things may have happened; our only clue is that there are two letters from Marten to Mary that can securely be dated late in the year 1661 and which show that the relationship had continued at least up to that point. Marten's removal to Berwick in July 1662 would have put paid to any future direct contact between them, unless Marten found a way of getting letters to her out of prison as successfully as he had managed while in the Tower of London. But who could have transported them? And could Mary have paid for them when they arrived?

Mary Ward (sometimes Mary Marten), along with Peggie, Poppet, and Bacon-hog, vanish from the record with the end of the surviving letters from Marten. All attempts to trace them further have proved fruitless. It is, sadly, impossible to do anything to confirm Sarah Barber's hopeful statement that 'Mary shared his imprisonment in Chepstow'.[36] It seems a good deal more probable that by the time the letters were published in Oxford in 1662 the relationship with Marten, which their publication had so wonderfully, if accidentally, celebrated, was already over.

One of Marten's tenderest letters to her had addressed the matter of life without him, and we can only hope that she did indeed get 'the offer ... of a new Dear', while paying attention to Marten's warnings 'especially of the fairest offers', for she had in the past been treated badly 'by such as were no mere strangers to thee'. We can only hope that the Mary Ward 'widow, about 28' who married 'William Burnett of Gray's Inn, gent., bachelor, about 30' on 5 November 1662,[37] was our Mary Ward, probably thirty-two rather than twenty-eight (she must have been born by 1630 and perhaps as early as 1624), but doubtless, with three children, claiming widowhood, and choosing not to be older than her husband ... who can say? But she was still 'My poor heart' when Marten wrote to her from the Tower: 'God be with my poor heart, and all the little pieces thereof' (L 8). His heart in pieces over her ... but his brats also pieces of his heart, also to be cherished.

It is in that run of tender wit that Marten is irresistible, as in his exclamations sent to Mary following a day in winter, 'starke staring mad from morning to night':

> Well (Love) it was happy turn that thou wert not here yes-
> terday, nor Peggie, nor Poppet, nor Bacon-hog, nor Dick, for
> I should have killed half a dozen of you at least, if you had
> come within my reach … (L 77)

For that day everything had gone wrong. Their messenger Dick Pettingall had been expected at the Tower first thing in the morning but had never arrived:

> and what servest thou for, but to have put him in mind of it,
> if he had forgot it? and what serves Peg for, but to put thee in
> minde of what thou fogettest? and what serves Poppet for, but
> to cry, and the tother to scold and scratch her mother when
> shee has forgotten? (L 77)

Via Dick, Marten could have sent her all kinds of things without paying a penny; as it was, he had not even had wood to heat his room so had had to buy some at an exorbitant price. And then some had arrived anyway. But now, the next day, his anger has died down, and

> my malice is pretty well abated towards thee and thy Camer-
> ades, because I hope you are all starved by this time either with
> cold or hunger; and therefore to shew I bore a little good will
> once, I have ordered some provision for thy executors, *viz.* a
> pound of cotten candles, and another of rush, two two-pennie
> loaves, two new rolls, a piece of butter to serve till to morrow,
> a leg of mutton: the next time they shall have something else.
> Mean while I am

My Dears Ghosts
Owne,
H. M. (L 77–8)

And it is all down to the meddling and prurient royalist
Edmund Gayton, eager to take advantage of Marten, happy to
fake letters supposedly written by Marten's rival, and extremely
keen to make some money for himself, that such a body of brilliant, intimate writing should have come down to us. It has some
claim to be the first collection of genuinely private letters ever
published in England. As ever, it is Marten who does the words.
Here he is telling Mary – without putting any weight of responsibility on to her – that, simply by wanting him to live, she keeps
him alive at the worst of times:

> if it were not complementing, that is for fear of seeming to
> complement, I would tell thee, that I would not live: I am sure
> I would not beg to live, but because I finde thou wouldst have
> me live ... (L 37)

And his final tender, thoughtful comment is:

> therefore good Soul, if ever thou hast a design of satisfying me
> (which I believe thou art never without) study how to satisfie
> thy own mind, and there lie I as quiet as a Lamb. (L 37)

So he believes himself not only attached to her, not only concerned for her, but inevitably and implicitly within her. It is,
though, hard to imagine this immensely companionable, clever,
contentious, irrepressible man lying 'as quiet as a Lamb', and she
must have smiled at the thought of it.

Notes

Preface

1   E.g. the report that 'The Parliament hath voted our late King's death to be murder' (John Langley to Sir R. Leveson, 3 May 1660, *Fifth Report of the Royal Commission on Historical Manuscripts*, Part I, Report and Appendix, 1876 [hereafter *HMS5A*], p. 181).

2   William L. Sachse, 'England's "Black Tribunal": An Analysis of the Regicide Court', *Journal of British Studies*, xii. no. 2 (May 1973), 76.

3   H. N. Brailsford, *The Levellers and the English Revolution*, ed. Christopher Hill (1961), p. 455.

4   Brailsford, *The Levellers and the English Revolution*, ed. Hill, p. 455.

5   [Richard Overton], *A Remonstrance of Many Thousand Citizens, and Other Free-born People of England, to Their Own House of Commons* (1646), pp. 4–5; the pamphlet was 'Burned by order of the Commons on May 22d, 1647'.

6   The cross of St George ('the kingdom's arms') under the window at the back – see Illustration 2 – replaced the royal coat of arms during the trial: see Jason Peacey, 'Reporting a Revolution: A Failed Propaganda Campaign', in *The Regicides and the Execution of Charles I*, ed. Jason Peacey (Basingstoke, 2001), p. 168. The double-shield in Illustration 1 is incorrect.

7   *Journal of the House of Commons* [hereafter *JHC*], 4 January 1649.

8   John Aubrey, *Brief Lives: with, An Apparatus for the Lives
     of Our English Mathematical Writers*, ed. Kate Bennett,
     2 Vols. (Oxford, 2015) [hereafter Aubrey], i. 340–1. If
     Illustration 5 shows Marten, the lace-tipped cravat over
     armour suggests a dandy.

9   Lely's double portrait of John Bradshaw and Hugh Peters
     was defaced with a later inscription stating that Bradshaw
     was 'of ye High Court of Justice y^t condemned Charles
     Ist to death' (Collection of Pictures, Helmingham Hall); a
     conservator at the National Portrait Gallery has however
     indicated that the 'now' on the Marten portrait is part of
     the original picture (John Rees, 'Henry Marten and The
     Levellers', Lecture at the National Portrait Gallery, 15 June
     2017).

10   [Arthur Annesley, Earl of Anglesey], *England's Confusion*
     (1659), p. 3; John Stubbs, *Reprobates: The Cavaliers of the
     English Civil War* (2011), p. 438.

11   *England's Confusion*, p. 3; *A Copy of a letter from an
     officer of the army in Ireland, to his Highness the Lord
     Protector, concerning his changing of the Government*
     (?1656), p. 10.

12   The word dates from the middle of the sixteenth century
     but from 1649 was primarily used for those responsible for
     Charles I's death.

13   John Langley to Sir Richard Leveson, 3 May 1660,
     HMC5A 181.

14   *A Hue and Cry After the High Court of Injustice* (1660),
     p. 8.

15   William Smith to John Langley, 30 June 1660, *HMC5A*
     205.

16   Stephen Charlton to Sir Richard Leveson, 16 June 1660,
     HMC5A 168.

17 Andrew Newport to Sir Richard Leveson, 16 June 1660, *HMC5A* 154.

18 William Smith to John Langley, 18 and 25 August 1660, *HMC5A* 174; Andrew Newport to Sir Richard Leveson, 23 August 1660, *HMC5A* 155.

19 Basil Duke Henning, *The History of the House of Commons, 1660–1690*, Vol. 1 (1983), 318.

20 *The Parliamentary or Constitutional History of England*, 24 Vols. (1760), Vol. xxii, 446, 448; Edmund Ludlow, *A Voyce from the Watch Tower, Part Five: 1660–1662*, ed. A. B. Worden, Camden Fourth Series, Vol. 21 (1978) [hereafter Ludlow *Voyce*], 166.

21 *The Diary of John Evelyn*, ed. E. S. de Beer, 6 Vols. (Oxford, 1955), iii. 258.

22 William Smith to John Langley, 25 August 1660, *HMC5A* 174.

23 Don Jordan and Michael Walsh, *The King's Revenge* (2012), p. 237.

24 Charles II, speech to parliament, House of Lords, 27 July 1660 (*JHC*).

25 First perhaps predicted in the 1649 royalist newsbook *Mercurius Pragmaticus (For King Charls II)*.

26 *Oroonoko, or, The Royal Slave … by Mrs. A. Behn* (1688), p. 155.

27 Ed. L. L. Knoppers (Oxford, 2012), p. 110.

28 Aubrey i. 340; James Shirley's play *Hide Parke* (1637) was 'presented … upon first opening of the Parke' and refers to 'the horse race' there and the betting (A2^r, E2^v, E3^r).

1. Marten

1 *Mr. Henry Martin His Speech in the House of Commons, Before his Departure Thence* (1648), pp. 1–2.

2 Quoted by Jason McElligott, 'The Politics of Sexual Libel:

Royalist Propaganda in the 1640s', *Huntington Library Quarterly*, lxvii, no. 1 (March 2004), 84; 'Stipony' was raisin wine with lemon juice and sugar (perhaps named after Stepney, in the East End of London), 'wagtails' were prostitutes. McElligott states that the attacks on Marten (83–4) reveal 'a deliberate pattern of associations linked to the truth but not reliant on it' (87) but fails to provide any evidence beyond speculation of what 'the truth' might be. Some apparent examples of Marten's behaviour (e.g. Henry Neville's *Newes from the New Exchange* of 1650, cited in Aubrey ii. 1224) are royalist scandal-mongering.

3   William Prynne, *A Breif Memento to the Present Unparliamentary Junto* (1649), p. 13.

4   Gilbert Burnet, *History of My Own Time*, ed. Osmund Airy, 2 Vols. (Oxford, 1897), i. 283; Mark Noble, *The Lives of the English Regicides*, 2 Vols. (1798), ii. 59–60.

5   Susan Wiseman, '"Adam, the Father of all Flesh": Porno-Political Rhetoric and Political Theory in and after the English Civil War', *Pamphlet Wars: Prose in the English Revolution*, ed. James Holstun (1992), p. 141; Melissa M. Mowry, *The Bawdy Politic in Stuart England, 1660–1714* (Aldershot, 2004), pp. 41, 42, 139; 'hypervirility' is abnormal, excessive machismo.

6   Aubrey ii. 1223, i. 340; Sarah Barber, 'Henry Marten', *Oxford Dictionary of National Biography* [hereafter *ODNB*].

7   Thomas Gower to John Langley, 15 January 1652, *HMC5A* 192.

8   Written from 'The Holy Lambe in Abingdon', 12 July 1654, University of Leeds, Brotherton Collection, Marten/Loder Symonds MSS, Vol. 89, f. 1.

9   'Mercurius Philalethes', *Select City Quæries: Discovering Several Cheats, Abuses and Subtilties of the City Bawds,*

Whores, and Trapanners (1660), p. 4; cf., about Marten,
'And Lustfull Aretine's bawdy Leaves are his Evangelist-a'
(*Ratts Rhimed to Death. Or, The Rump-Parliament
Hang'd Up in the Shambles*, 1659, p. 50).

10   [John Phillips], *Montelion* (1660), n. p.; *A Perfect Diurnall
or the Daily Proceedings in the Conventicle of the
Phanatiques* (1659) [1660], p. 7; *The Fifth and Last Part of
the Wandring Whore a Dialogue* (1661), pp. 14, 12.

11   [Phillips], *Montelion*, n. p.

12   I.e. one who attacked the Church of England: cf.
'Roundheads, Sectaries, Schismaticks, and what not?'
(Thomas Hubbert, *A Pill to Purge Formality*, 1650, p.
34); cf. 'Against our late Schismatics', *The Diary of John
Evelyn*, ed. de Beer, iv. 131.

13   *A Declaration Concerning Colonel Henry Martin,
Colonel Robert Lilburn, Colonel Downs* (1660), p. 4; the
pamphlet's error in reporting that John Barkstead had
been imprisoned (p. 5) suggests that it was put together
late in August or early in September 1660. Cross Lane
was notorious in the Restoration period, as in William
Boghurst's 1666 reference to 'the common *hackney
prostitutes* of Luten Lane, Dog Yard, *Cross Lane*' in
Loimographia (1894), p. 96.

14   *A Free-Parliament-Letany* (1660), n. p.

15   'A quarrel betwixt Tower-Hill and Tiburne', *Merry
Drollery, or A Collection of Jovial Poems, Merry Songs,
Witty Drolleries Intermix'd with Pleasant Catches /
Collected by W. N., C. B., R. S., J. G., Lovers of Wit*
(1661), p. 124.

16   Aubrey i. 341; the deletion is Aubrey's.

17   Stephen Charlton to John Langley, 13 November 1660,
HMC5A 169.

18   Christopher Hill, *God's Englishman: Oliver Cromwell and the English Revolution* (Harmondsworth, 1972), p. 53.

19   *JHC* 3 December 1641.

20   Aubrey i. 341.

21   *His Maiesties Declaration to All His Loving Subjects of the 12 of August 1642* (York, reprinted Oxford, 1642), pp. 71, 89, 90.

22   Anthony Wood offers one anecdote he did not get from Aubrey: Marten is supposed to have been '*authorized by the said Parliament* about 1642' to open a great iron Chest within the College of *Westminster*, and thence took out the Crown, Robes, Sword and Scepter belonging antiently to K. *Edw.* the Confessor, and used by all our Kings at their inaugurations; and with a scorn greater than his lusts and the rest of his vices, he openly declared that *there should be no further use of these toyes and trifles*, &c. And in the jollity of that humour he invested *George Wither* (an old puritan Satyrist) in the royal habiliments: who, being crown'd and royally arrayed (as well right became him) did first march about the room with a stately garb, and afterwards with a thousand apish and rediculous actions exposed those sacred ornaments to contempt and laughter. (*Athenae Oxonienses*, 2 Vols., 1691–2, ii. 493)
      1642 would have been very early for such an assault on the apparatus of royalty. Wood's source is unknown, and I am inclined to question its authenticity; the comments on Marten's 'lusts and the rest of his vices' simply recycle old rumour.

23   Aubrey i. 341–2. The anecdote was perhaps repeated in 1659 by Arthur Annesley in his reference to 'Single hearted, preaching Sir *Henry Vane*, now become old Sir *Harry*' (*England's Confusion*, p. 10).

24   Aubrey i. 342.

25   *OED* suggests: 'In reference to the light sleeping of dogs, and the difficulty of telling whether, when their eyes are shut, they are asleep or not.'

26   Aubrey i. 341–2.

27   Sarah Barber, *A Revolutionary Rogue: Henry Marten and the English Republic* (Thrupp, 2000) [hereafter Barber (2000)], p. 6; *Three Speeches Delivered at a* Common-Hall, *on Saturday 28 July 1643* (1643), p. 18.

28   Quoted in John Rees, *The Leveller Revolution* (2016), p. 89.

29   Aubrey i. 341.

30   Edward Hyde, Earl of Clarendon, *The life of Edward Earl of Clarendon*, 3 Vols. (Oxford, 1759), i. 81–2.

31   Hyde, *The Life of Edward Earl of Clarendon*, i. 82; C. M. Williams, 'The Anatomy of a Radical Gentleman / Henry Marten', *Puritans and Revolutionaries*, ed. Donald Pennington and Keith Thomas (Oxford, 1978) [hereafter Williams], p. 137.

32   *Mercurius Aulicus* (19 August 1643), p. 452; David R. Como, *Radical Parliamentarians and the English Civil War* (Oxford, 2018), p. 177.

33   *Mercurius Aulicus* (19 August 1643), p. 452, is the only original source available for Pym's remark; *JHC* reports 'an expunged Entry' in the original journal.

34   *A Letter sent to LONDON from a Spie at OXFORD* (Oxford, 1643), p. 6.

35   William Walwyn, *Juries Justified: or, a Word of Correction to Mr. Henry Robinson* (1651), p. 3.

36   Sarah Barber, 'A Bastard Kind of Militia', *Soldiers, Writers and Statesmen of the English Revolution*, ed. Ian Gentles, John Morrill and Blair Worden (Cambridge, 1998), p. 138.

37   Barber (2000), p. 9; Rees, *The Leveller Revolution*, p. 94.

38   Barber, 'A Bastard Kind of Militia', p. 138.

Illustration 20: Henry Marten: engraving, *c.* 1799

39 Williams 121.

40 The work corresponds to the description of a painting in
    the Lewis family house at St Pierre, near Chepstow, given
    in Charles Heath's *Historical and Descriptive Accounts
    of the Ancient and Present State of the Town and Castle
    of Chepstow* (Monmouth, 1801), pp. [89–92]. It remains
    possible that it is the painting of a Lewis ancestor;
    questions have also been raised about the period of the
    cravat in the painting and about the painting of the boy.
    An engraving of the portrait appeared as 'Henry Martin'
    in Coxe ii. opp. 381 but was described in Heath's book as
    'so *unlike the original*, that it might serve as well for any
    other person as for Harry Marten' (p. [92]).

41   *A Word to Mr Wil. Prynn Esq. and Two for the Parliament and Army* (1649), p. 15 (although dated '1649' the pamphlet was written before the decision had been taken to put the king on trial: Thomason dated his copy '6 Jan').

42   *A Word to Mr Wil. Prynn Esq.*, pp. 16, 7.

43   *A Declaration of the Parliament of England, Expressing the Grounds of Their Late Proceedings, and of Setling the Present Government in the Way of a Free State* (1649), p. 20.

44   Barber (2000), pp. 95–119.

45   Barber (2000), p. 96.

46   Aubrey i. 341.

47   Aubrey i. 342.

48   The thirteen members were Oliver Cromwell; Major-Generals John Lambert, Thomas Harrison, John Desborough and Matthew Thomlinson; Colonels Anthony Stapley, Robert Bennet, William Sydenham and Philip Jones; and four civilians, Walter Strickland, Sir Gilbert Pickering, John Carew and Samuel Moyer.

49   [Edward Sexby], *Killing No Murder: Briefly Discoursed in Three Questions* (1657), p. 13; cited in Blair Worden, *Literature and Politics in Cromwellian England* (Oxford, 2007), p. 113. Marten's surprise was reimagined in the ballad 'The House Out of Doors … Another on the Same': 'Harry Martin wonder'd to see such a thing, / Done by a Saint of so high a degree; / An Act which he did not expect from a King' (*The Rump, or a Collection of Songs and Ballads, Made Upon Those Who Would Be a Parliament, and Were But the Rump of an House of Commons, Five Times Dissolv'd, 1660, p. 22*).

50   Marten/Loder-Symonds MSS, Political and Miscellaneous, Vol. 2, 1651–8, fol. 12; Marten/Loder Symonds MSS, Vol. 93, ff. 2–4v, 39–40v; Barber (2000) 38.

51 Aubrey i. 341; see Preface.

52 David Norbrook, *Writing the English Republic: Poetry, Rhetoric and Politics, 1627–1660* (Cambridge, 1999), p. 317.

53 Norbrook, *Writing the English Republic*, p. 496.

54 Barber, 'Henry Marten', *ODNB*.

55 John Jorden to Marten, n.d., Historical Manuscripts Commission, 'The manuscripts of Capt. F. C. Loder-Symonds', in *The Manuscripts of Rye and Hereford Corporations*, pp. 378–404: *British History Online* http://www.british-history.ac.uk/hist-mss-comm/vol31/pt4/pp378–404 [accessed 8 November 2020].

56 John Price, *The Mystery and Method of His Majesty's Happy Restauration, Laid Open to Publick View* (1680), pp. 151–2.

2. Tower

1 None of the letters is dated and very few allow an exact date to be ascribed. An exception is letter no. 34, which describes how the Speaker of the House of Commons 'takes Physick for ten dayes' and how 'tomorrow is Saturday' (*L* 31) – showing that the letter was written on Friday, 13 January 1660, the day Speaker William Lenthall (1591–1662) absented himself because he was ill.

2 Thomas Gower to Sir Richard Leveson, 14 August 1660, *HMC5A* 195.

3 I.e. 'eking out' (the *Oxford English Dictionary* [hereafter *OED*] $v.^4$ offers examples of 'etch out' – meaning 'eke out' – from 1682 and 1698. The 1662–3 editions print 'ietching out' (*L* 2): a misprint or a personal idiom.

4 Marten would have known that, when assassinated, Dorislaus (1595–1649) was serving as a judge of the High

Court of Admiralty, the position Marten's father had occupied 1618–41.

5   *The Diary of Samuel Pepys*, ed. R. Latham and W. Matthews, 11 Vols. (1970–83), iv. 77–8; a bufflehead (first recorded 1659) is a fool or blockhead.

6   *Memoirs of the Life of Colonel Hutchinson*, ed. Julius Hutchinson and C. H. Firth (1906), p. 364.

7   *Memoirs of the Life of Colonel Hutchinson*, ed. Hutchinson and Firth, p. 354.

8   'Articles and Ordinances' [Appendix to Part II], John Bayley, *The History and Antiquities of the Tower of London*, 2 Vols. (1825), ii. cxi-cxii.

9   *Memoirs of the Life of Colonel Hutchinson*, ed. Hutchinson and Firth, p. 355.

10 Jane Marten to Marten, 31 March [1657], Historical Manuscripts Commission, 'The manuscripts of Capt. F. C. Loder-Symonds', in *The Manuscripts of Rye and Hereford Corporations*, pp. 378–404: *British History Online* http://www.british-history.ac.uk/hist-mss-comm/vol31/pt4/pp378–404 [accessed 8 November 2020].

11 *Memoirs of the Life of Colonel Hutchinson*, ed. Hutchinson and Firth, p. 364.

12 In communist Czechoslovakia prisoners were billed for maintenance during their stay in prison: the dissident Jiří Wolf (b. 1952), for e.g., was in December 1989 'still technically in debt to the state for 4,200 crowns for the privilege of six years' brutal punishment' (Graham Swift, *Making an Elephant*, 2009, p. 178).

13 Worden, *Literature and Politics in Cromwellian England*, p. 74.

14 Wood, *Athenae Oxonienses*, ii. 174; cf. John Wilkins, *Of the Principles and Duties of Natural Religion*, Book II (1675), pp. 285–6; Williams 125.

15 Aubrey i. 340.

16 Williams 125–6.

17 Blair Worden, *Roundhead Reputations* (2001), pp. 61, 292.

18 *The Speeches and Prayers of Some of the Late King's Judges* (1660), p. 56.

3. Tending and Scribbling

1 https://www.goodreads.com/book/show/4177326.

2 Aubrey i. 341.

3 Jeremy Boulton, 'Food Prices and the Standard of Living in London in the "Century of Revolution", 1580–1700', *The Economic History Review*, New Series, Vol. 53, No. 3 (Aug. 2000), 459, reports the cost of flour 1600–10 as being on average at 52d per bushel – and prices were no lower in the 1660s.

4 Barber (2000) 106.

5 *OED* 8a.

6 Aubrey ii. 1223.

4. Procedures

1 Geoffrey Robertson, *The Tyrannicide Brief* (2005), pp. 306 and 407–8 points out an omission in *EIA* of material in the *Parliamentary Intelligencer*, no. 43, p. 660.

2 See *OED* n$^{1.}$ 2.b.; misunderstood by e.g. Robertson (p. 5) and Jordan and Walsh (p. 225), who refer to the 'Death Hum' as if it were an actual humming sound.

3 William Hewlet was added during the trial, bringing the number up to the 'Twenty nine' claimed on the title page of *EIA*.

4 *The Proceedings at the Sessions House in the Old-Baily, London on Thursday the 24th day of November, 1681* (1681), pp. 12–48.

5   *The Diary of Samuel Pepys*, ed. Latham and Matthews, i. 263.

6   *OED* 22.a.III.

7   *The Proceedings at the Sessions House in the Old-Baily, London on Thursday the 24th Day of November, 1681*, pp. 38, 39, 48.

8   Gerald Howson, *Thief-Taker General: Jonathan Wild and the Emergence of Crime and Corruption* (Oxford, 1970), p. 27.

9   *A Looking-Glass for Traytors*, p. [1].

10 The wooden frame (or sledge) on which traitors would be drawn through the streets to execution (*OED* 1.c.).

11 *The Diary of Samuel Pepys*, ed. Latham and Matthews, i. 265.

12 David Cannadine, *Dethroning Historical Reputations* (2018), p. 8.

13 *The Diary of John Evelyn*, ed. de Beer, iii. 259.

14 Prynne, *A Breif Memento*, p. 4.

15 Robertson, *The Tyrannicide Brief*, p. 337, describes the entrails being dragged out with tongs through the anus. All existing images of the procedure show the body sliced open to below the navel, for no good reason if the anus were being used for the extraction.

16 William Smith to John Langley, 20 October 1660, *HMC5A* 174.

17 'The Tragedie of Macbeth', II. ii. (1623), p. 136.

18 *The Diary of Samuel Pepys*, ed. Latham and Matthews, i. 269–70.

19 *The Diary of John Evelyn*, ed. de Beer, iii. 259.

5. Old Bailey

1   Marten uses the common terminology of those attempting to explain that, although not supporters of a regime, they

nevertheless had to acknowledge its authority: cf. Oliver St. John's declaration that, although chief justice, he was 'Commanded by those who then, *de facto,* though not *de jure,* exercised the Supream Power of the Nation' (*The Case of Oliver St. John, Esq., Concerning His Actions During the Late Troubles,* 1660, p. 9).

2   J. R. Tanner, *English Constitutional Conflicts of the Seventeenth Century 1603–1689* (Cambridge, 1928), p. 214.

3   Ludlow *Voyce* 219–20.

4   The House of Commons on 10 February 1646 had resolved that 'Thanks be given to Major-General *Browne,* for his great Services, faithfully performed to the Parliament and Kingdom, in his Care of *Abingdon,* and other his good Services.'

5   David Masson, *The Life of John Milton,* 6 Vols. (Edinburgh, 1880), vi. 10.

6   [Annesley], *England's Confusion,* p. 10.

7   Jordan and Walsh, *The King's Revenge,* pp. 172–3.

8   Andrew Newport to Sir Richard Leveson, 12 May 1660; Thomas Langley to Sir Richard Leveson, 7 June 1660 and 16 June 1660, *HMC5A* 207.

9   Thomas Scot – who had also handed himself in – had fled the country in April 1660 but 'was persuaded to surrender himself to Sir Henry de Vic, the king's resident at Brussels, in the hope of saving his life by thus obeying the royal proclamation for the surrender of the regicides'. He had nevertheless not handed himself in to the Serjeant at Arms by 20 June, and his lack of repentance counted against him: as late as March 1660 he had remarked 'that he desired no better epitaph than "Here lies one who had a hand and a heart in the execution of Charles Stuart"' (Sean Kelsey, 'Thomas Scot', *ODNB*).

10 William Allen, *A Faithful Memorial of that Remarkable Meeting of Many Officers* (1659), p. 5. The opposite would also be argued: cf. the title of a pamphlet by Fabian Philipps, *King Charles the First, No Man of Blood: But a Martyr for His People* (1649).

11 Numbers xxxv. 33.

12 A. L. Rowse, *Four Caroline Portraits* (1993), p. 87.

13 W. Smith to John Langley, 7 June 1660, *HMC5A* 207; *JHC* 21 May 1660.

14 The 11th edition of the *Encyclopaedia Britannica*, 29 Vols. (1910–11) recorded in its entry on 'Drawing and Quartering' 'a tradition that Harrison the regicide', fighting to the end, 'after being disembowelled, rose and boxed the ears of the executioner' (viii. 557).

15 *A Looking-Glass for Traytors*, p. [1].

16 Andrew Newport to Sir Richard Leveson, 11 October 1660, *HMC5A* 157.

17 Andrew Newport to Sir Richard Leveson, 11 October 1660, *HMC5A* 157.

18 In 1662, Robert Ewer and Richard Ewer paid hearth tax in Bicester (Market End), and on 10 January 1680, Robert Ewer (shopkeeper), of Farrington, Berkshire, married Jane Austell, daughter of William of Ore. The Berkshire connection is intriguing for someone who might have been one of Marten's servants.

19 Hill, *God's Englishman*, p. 185; Barber (2000), p. 162. Sir Charles Firth, in *Oliver Cromwell and the Rule of the Puritans in England* (1900), however, ignored it.

20 *The Memoirs of Edmund Ludlow*, ed. Firth, ii. 325. The words do not appear in Ludlow *Voyce*; the Whig political defender John Toland (1670–1722) probably wrote them. See Ludlow *Voyce* 22–80 and Blair Worden, 'Whig History and Puritan Politics: The *Memoirs* of Edmund Ludlow

Revisited', *Historical Research*, Vol. 75 (May 2002), 209–37.

6. 'My last and onely Love'

1   Historical Manuscripts Commission, 'The manuscripts of Capt. F. C. Loder-Symonds', in *The Manuscripts of Rye and Hereford Corporations,* pp. 378–404. *British History Online* http://www.british-history.ac.uk/hist-mss-comm/vol31/pt4/pp378–404 [accessed 8 November 2020].

2   Edward Gower to Sir Richard Leveson, 10 November 1660, *HMC5A* 200. Gower confuses Marten with his father, as did Cromwell (see p. 19).

3   Stephen Charlton to Sir Richard Leveson, 15 May 1660, *HMC5A* 205.

4   Andrew Newport to Sir Richard Leveson, 13 November 1660, *HMC5A* 157.

5   Stephen Charlton to Sir Richard Leveson, 13 November 1660, *HMC5A* 169.

6   Thomas Gower to John Langley, 20 November 1660, *HMC5A* 195; Edward Gower to Sir Richard Leveson, 8 December 1660, *HMC5A* 201.

7   *The Parliamentary or Constitutional History of England,* 24 Vols. (1761), xxiii. 42.

8   Ludlow *Voyce* 160, 153.

9   *A Word to Mr Wil. Prynn Esq.,* pp. 3–5.

10   *The Diary of Samuel Pepys,* ed. Latham and Matthews, ii. 85.

11   Edward Gower to Sir Richard Leveson, 18 May 1661, *HMC5A* 203.

12   *L* 34 prints 'shin-and bone'.

13   Cf. 'A kept Mistress too! my bowels yearn to her already' (John Dryden, *The Kind Keeper; or Mr Limberham,* 1680, p. 5).

14 Graham Swift, *The Light of Day* (2003), p. 108.

7. Commons

1 James Heath, *A Brief Chronicle of the Late Intestine Warr in the Three Kingdoms of England, Ireland and Scotland* (1663), p. 468.

2 *The Loyall Martyrology ... with the Catalogue and Characters of Those Regicides Who Sat as Judges on Our Late Dread Soveraign of Ever Blessed Memory* (1665), pp. 113–14; Heath, *A Brief Chronicle of the Late Intestine Warr*, p. 367.

3 Ludlow *Voyce* 294–5; the 'poor lambes' are not sentimental but biblical (cf. John i. 29, Revelation v. 6–14): cf. 'those poore innocent lambes of Christ' (Ludlow *Voyce* 197).

4 *JHC* 18–19 April 1643; *The Parliamentary or Constitutional History of England*, 24 Vols. (1753), xii. 238–40.

5 Thomas May, *The History of the Parliament of England, Which Began November the Third 1640* (1812), p. 120; David L. Smith, *Constitutional Royalism and the Search for Settlement*, Cambridge, 1994, p. 187.

6 In 1655, Cromwell would have a new Great Seal made, one side showing him (from 26 December 1653 lord protector) on horseback, the other side showing the Commonwealth coat of arms (incorporating English, Irish, and Scottish flags), with Latin inscriptions on both sides, thus returning England and Ireland to (and bringing Scotland under) the authority of a single, named, horse-riding ruler, its coat of arms (supported by a crowned lion) surmounted by a royal helm and a crown and crest, circumscribed by the old language of the ruling elite.

7   Bulstrode Whitelocke, *Memorials of the English Affairs* (1682), p. 362.

8   Of the original 1648/9 Seal, damaged impressions survive: see A. B. and A. Wyon, *The Great Seals of England* (1887), pp. 88–93. See, too, Sean Kelsey, *Inventing a Republic: The Political Culture of the English Commonwealth* (Manchester, 1997), pp. 93–7.

9   Aubrey i. 535, 341: cf. 'from his mother's womb' (Acts iii. 2 and xiv. 8), 'a man which was blind from his birth' (John ix. 1) and 'he was restored, and saw every man clearly' (Mark viii. 25).

10   Roger Coke, *A Detection of the Court and State of England During the Four Last Reigns, and the Inter-Regnum*, 2 Vols. (1696), i. 415. Elaborations have been offered – e.g. 'Henry Marten moved an amendment that the "Lords were useless, but not dangerous," but he withdrew this derisive suggestion and the motion was carried' (Ivor Waters, *Henry Marten and the Long Parliament*, Chepstow, 1973, p. 47) – but none appears to originate in the seventeenth century. *JHC* shows that the only vote taken had been on 5 February 1649, when 'the Question' was put "That this House shall take the Advice of the House of Lords, in the Exercise of the Legislative Power"', which was lost 29 to 44 (Marten being a teller for the 'noes'). On the 6th the wording abolishing the Lords was not voted on but '*Resolved, &c*'.

8. Lords

1   *A True and Humble Representation of John Downes Esq; Touching the Death of the Late King* (1660), p. [1].

2   Ludlow *Voyce* 295.

3   Heath, *A Brief Chronicle of the Late Intestine Warr*, p. 468.

4   Tanner, *English Constitutional Conflicts of the
     Seventeenth Century*, p. 102.
5   *JHC* 17 August 1660.
6   It has been stated that they were taken prisoner in 1661
     (Worden, *Roundhead Reputations*, p. 50), but the seizure
     was only technically in 1661, being before 25 March.
7   T. B. Howell, *A Complete Collection of State Trials and
     Proceedings for High Treason*, 21 Vols. (1816), v. 1306.
8   Andrew Newport to Sir Richard Leveson, 16 August 1660,
     HMC5A 155.
9   Mowry, *The Bawdy Politic*, p. 39.
10   Waters, *Henry Marten and the Long Parliament*, p. 66.
11   Davenant wrote to Marten from the Tower on 8 July 1652:
     'I would it were worthy of you to know how often I have
     profess'd that I had rather owe my libertie to you than to
     any man, and that the obligation you lay upon me shall for
     ever be acknowledg'd' (ML v93/11, Brotherton Collection,
     University of Leeds).
12   Barber, 'Henry Marten', *ODNB*.
13   Burnet, *History of My Own Time*, ed. Airy, i. 282–3; see
     too Barber (2000) 163.
14   Aubrey i. 341.
15   Forster, *Lives of Eminent British Statesmen*, p. 357.
16   *The Rule and Exercises of Holy Dying* (1651), p. 16.
17   Barber, 'Henry Marten', *ODNB*; J. T. Peacey and Ivan
     Roots, 'John Downes', *ODNB*; Gordon Goodwin, 'John
     Downes', *DNB*; *A True and Humble Representation of
     John Downes Esq*, p. [1].
18   *Memoirs of the Life of Colonel Hutchinson*, ed.
     Hutchinson and Firth, pp. 361, 368–70, 363.

9. Ghostless in Chepstow

1   Waters, *Henry Marten and the Long Parliament*, p. 71.

2   *JHC* 21 December 1666 and 17 January 1667.

3   Aubrey i. 341.

4   Stephen Charlton to Sir Richard Leveson, 1 May 1660;
    HMC5A 167.

5   Details from John Clifford Perks, *Chepstow Castle* (1967),
    pp. 10–12; *JHC* 21 May 1660.

6   The Reverend Stebbing Shaw, *A Tour to the West of
    England, in 1788* (1789), p. 222.

7   Aubrey i. 341.

8   Such care is invented in *The Story of Henry Marten*,
    ed. Alan Hicks and David Lewis (Oxford, 1993): 'She
    visited him regularly, finally moving in with Henry in a
    comfortable prison apartment, with two maids resident
    above' (p. 13). Hicks and Lewis are indebted to Coxe,
    ii. 389.

9   Jane Marten to Marten, 31 March [1657].

10 Wood, *Athenae Oxonienses*, ii. 494.

11 Aubrey i. 341.

12 Heath, *Historical and Descriptive Accounts*, p. [86].

13 *The Life and Times of Anthony Wood, Antiquary, of
    Oxford, 1632–1695, Described by Himself*, ed. Andrew
    Clark, 5 Vols. (Oxford, 1891–1900), ii. 504.

14 Heath, *Historical and Descriptive Accounts*, pp. [82–3].

15 Charles Heath, *Monmouthshire: Descriptive Accounts of
    Persfield and Chepstow* (Monmouth, 1793), p. 30.

16 Heath, *Historical and Descriptive Accounts*, p. [76].

17 '*Catherine married Mr. Badham, a mason, who came
    from Monmouth, and lived at the house at the end of the
    bridge. Margaret married Mr. Heyworth, who kept an
    Inn, and lived at what is now called Pye Corner*' (Heath,
    Historical and Descriptive Accounts, p. [76]).

18 Heath, *Historical and Descriptive Accounts*, p. [76].

19 See pp. 15–16 and note 40, Chapter 1.

20   Heath, *Historical and Descriptive Accounts*, pp. [76–7].

21   Aubrey ii. 1223.

22   By his second wife, Thomas Morgan of Llansoy fathered Henry Morgan of Caerleon (b. 1644); and the latter would appear to be the Henry Morgan of Caerleon Usk listed as a JP for the county of Monmouthshire in 1683.

23   Bayntun (1618–79) was an MP at various times before and after 1660.

24   Aubrey i. 341; see ii. 1226 for information about Bayntun and drinking.

25   Wood, *Athenae Oxonienses*, ii. 495.

26   James Baker, *A Picturesque Guide Through Wales and the Marches; Interspersed with the Most Interesting Subjects of Antiquity in That Principality* (Worcester, 1795), p. 25.

27   *Examen Poeticum: Being the Third Part of Miscellany Poems* (1693), p. 396.

28   Heath, *Historical and Descriptive Accounts*, pp. [78–9].

29   Norbrook, *Writing the English Republic: Poetry, Rhetoric and Politics, 1627–1660*, p. 495; Williams 127.

30   Wood, *Athenae Oxonienses*, ii. 495.

31   *Sepulchrorum Inscriptiones: Or a Curious Collection of Above 900 of the Most Remarkable Epitaphs*, 2 Vols. (1727), i. 165.

32   Williams 129.

33   John Lilburne, *Rash Oaths Unwarrantable* (1647), p. 1.

34   Williams 138; *Mercurius Pragmaticus*, 22–29 August 1648.

35   Aubrey i. 341; cited in Worden, *Literature and Politics in Cromwellian England*, p. 76; *The Parliaments Proceedings Justified, in Declining a Personall Treaty with the King*, p. 3.

36   Barber, 'Henry Marten', *ODNB*; cf. *The Story of Henry Marten*, ed. Hicks and Lewis: 'Mary Ward … might well have been with him at the end' (p. 13).

37 *London Marriage Licences 1521–1869*, ed. Joseph Foster (1887), p. 220.

Index

Page numbers in **bold** denote illustrations; relationships (in brackets) are to Henry Marten (hereafter HM).